Published in California, United States
Printed in the USA

Awakening at Home
www.awakeningathome.org

Connect with us through Awakening at Home awakeningathome@gmail.com

Print ISBN: 979-8-9863361-3-8
Digital ISBN: 979-8-9863361-0-7

Jacqueline's *Awakening at Home* distills the essence of the wisdom gained in her decades long Buddhist meditation, her experience as a Mom, and her personal growth. This book is very accessible, helpful, and inspirational for anyone wanting to connect with themselves spiritually and bring peace to their heart.

~ **Lama Palden**

Jacqueline offers profound Dharma accessible to us seekers who are ordinary householders. She speaks directly to our hearts with her vivid accounts and authentic, yet artistic, analyses of our resistance to get to the pillow and stay seated until the bell rings.This book offers compassionate support to "find happiness where we are"— even in illness, as we learn from Jacqueline's first-hand experiences. Jacqueline has beautifully integrated and skillfully shared her reflections as a mother, meditator, and meditation teacher.

~ **Christie Chang**
Former Sakyadhita International President

Awakening at Home poignantly offers the depth of guidance many of us seek. With healing insights, Jacqueline models how to transform a home into a temple. Reading this book feels like being listened to and understood by a wise and loving woman.

~ **Paula Arai, Ph.D.**
Author of *Women Living Zen*,
Bringing Zen Home and *Painting Enlightenment*

If you are looking for a book on how to live a spiritual life daily, look no longer. *Awakening At Home* finds no mundane activity or task that is outside the path—from driving in traffic to cooking dinner to walking in the neighborhood. How much can we include in our field of awareness? What are we excluding? How do we deepen our attention in order to reap the fruits of a life lived fully moment by moment? Kramer reminds us that we are not monks or hermit sages, but householders with jobs, families, and a world of attachments—and waking up is possible everywhere and at all times.

~ **Roshi Eve Myonen Marko**
Founding Teacher, Zen Peacemaker Order
Founding Teacher, Green River Zen Center

In gratitude for all the women and men

everywhere who are creating a kinder world

Table of Contents

Introduction

The afternoon wind is blowing through the maple tree in my front yard, stirring up dust devils on the street. It may just be a June wind, but I hear it faintly whisper, *the climate is changing*. After living in this home for over 40 years, I've come to know the sighs and mutters of the trees and birds and bushes in this fruitful and life-sustaining Sonoma valley.

Thirty-eight years ago I sat in this same room listening to what felt like a less menacing wind create music through the wind chimes. Pregnant and about to begin a journey that would take me through divorce, illness, teachings, and openings. This is where I had those first unexpected insights into the transformative power of motherhood. Then I traveled through a book, a non-profit, students, and numerous essays and talks. From my current vantage point it seems like I was being dragged, kicking and screaming, through the whole experience. But something was moving through me, just as the wind is moving through the maple tree right now. I had no power to contain it. What I was learning did not feel like my wisdom—just as the tree does not make the wind that moves through its leaves and branches. It just responds to the wind. I just responded to what I was learning.

I wrote *Buddha Mom* during those years of active motherhood. In it I shared my journey from pregnancy to birthing to motherhood as reflected in the light of classical Buddhist practice and goddess wisdom. At the time, and to this day, I love digging my bare hands in dark soil and watching bees buzz around flowers. Back to the land, simple life, Thoreau, sustainability and home-centered feminine wisdom seasoned with Zen thought and practice. This was just my personal journey.

I came to learn that, while writing *Buddha Mom*, I was in a state of Zen sickness, although I didn't know that term at the time. Zen sickness is the evangelical zeal expressed after a powerful spiritual opening. If you have a teacher who knows about Zen sickness, they tell you to cool your jets and just keep practicing. I had no such teacher at the time so my sickness went on, unabated, for many years. I was excited about the joy the teachings brought me and wished it for everyone. I've since learned that we are each called to a unique, hand-made life. This book in your hands now is an attempt to express the same insights written about in *Buddha Mom* but from a different perspective.

After 43 years of mothering, 20 years of grand mothering, a move from an orthodox form of Buddhism through an unorthodox form of Zen, and then back out again into the land of spiritual but not religious, I'm ready to speak of these insights from a more expansive view of what is possible, to hopefully create the space for you, dear reader, to find your own path to awakening. Although my Zen sickness has subsided, I still feel a strong call to honor mothers, to write about their heroic journeys from the one to the many, and to share practices that support a more fluid, happy experience on the path.

The home is where we learn to love and where we learn to fear. How we raise our children is the imprint we make on the culture around us. As countries build greater arsenals of nuclear weapons and greed threatens the preservation of this one planet we call home, we need to address the imbalance in the world on many fronts. It is just as important to address the climate in the home as it is to address the climate of the planet if we're to create a sane world.

Buddha Mom focused on Buddhism, this book reflects on the same insights but from a broader perspective. When the Buddha was asked what gave him the authority to teach, he placed his hand on the Earth. All Dharma, all wisdom, is available right where we are. This little book is built around the Buddha's teaching that awakening can happen in four positions: sitting, walking, standing, and lying down. I think the Buddha must have had a wonderful sense of humor to limit the positions one can awaken in to all positions. To me this teaching says we can awaken wherever we are, which includes in the home.

I have been blessed with many wonderful teachers, rooms full of books, and practices that have allowed me to experience these teachings first hand. I don't belong to any school of Buddhism, or any Judeo-Christian school, although I honor and have the deepest respect for all these traditions. But here, in this living room in the late afternoon, the wind is as much my teacher as all these words and practices.

Whatever mothers or fathers there be,
single or married,
Gay, straight, or celibate,
African, Asian, Middle Eastern, Indigenous, or European,
Those dwelling near or in far off lands,
Those who give birth and those who nurture
already-birthed children,
May all beings, without exception, be happy minded.
Let not one parent judge another,
Nor be unkind to any person whatever, in any place,
In anger or ill will, let us not wish another harm.
Just as a parent protects their only child,
Even at risk to their own life,
Let our thoughts of boundless love pervade the whole world,
Above, below, and across,
Without any obstruction
Without any hatred
Without any enmity
Whether we sit, stand, walk or lie down,
As long as we are awake,
Let us develop awareness.
This, they say, is the way to true happiness.

(Variation on the Metta Sutta)

Sitting

We start our journey of transformation with personal awakening. Daily sitting practice is a time-tested way to become more intimate with our inner workings. We awaken within the privacy of our own unique mind. We listen to ourselves and we hear the universe.

Most spiritual practice instruction has been based on monastic traditions where a group sits together at prescribed times. What might a dedicated spiritual practice look like in the home? What challenges are there? How is sitting in silence and stillness different from practicing mindfulness while taking a bath, running, or chopping vegetables? How is it the same?

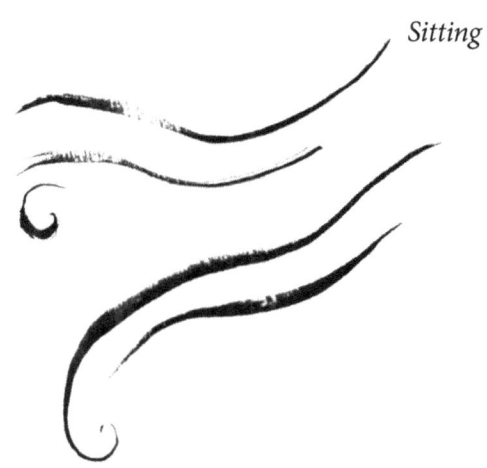

True meditation has no direction, goals, or method. All methods aim at achieving a certain state of mind. All states are limited, impermanent and conditioned. Fascination with states leads only to bondage and dependency. True meditation is abidance as primordial consciousness.

Adyashanti

WHY SIT?

Outside my room a bell rings. It's 5:30 in the morning and the awakener is walking up and down the hall striking a gong, calling dreamers to leave their warm beds, dress, throw some water on their faces and walk the chilly path to the meditation hall. In the dark hall ghostly figures file in, illuminated by the dim light of candles surrounding the parameter of the hall. Each person's spot is a nest of pillows and blankets lined up against the wall. As the last of the meditators enter and cocoon themselves in their spot, the energy in the hall settles down to a deep quiet. We become one body as we share the first sit of the morning. As the days progress we each travel through our own private heavens and hells. Boredom, excitement, anger, bliss, pain, fear, lust, love and more, coloring what appears on the outside to be blissful stillness. At the end of our time together we are all fundamentally changed, then tossed out into a world that is a lot less sensitive than we've become. What now?

For many years I went on a meditation retreat at least once each year. Even when my daughter was very young and I was single I found a way to join a group to enliven my practice. To go on retreat costs time and money, time and money that would have gone into vacations and entertainment. Not everyone has the discretionary income or wants to spend their hard earned money on a meditation retreat. But it was a priority to me. Retreat recharged my batteries and made the difficult not only bearable but alive and meaningful. Returning home after retreat I faced the challenge of maintaining the strides I had made, now within the complexity of daily life. Sitting at home is a very different challenge than sitting for an extended period of time with a group. Although the challenges are different, I discovered that the benefits of both are considerable and worth the effort.

We are beginning our exploration of awakening at home with sitting meditation because sitting in silence is a craft worth cultivating. When we sit in silence we have the opportunity to be aware of what we are feeling, thinking and sensing in the moment without having to evaluate or act on our experience. This simple awareness has the power to open up worlds of insight and freedom that follow us into our everyday activities. Meditation drills down below the surface of our awareness and guides our everyday mindfulness practice into deeper and deeper layers.

Sitting meditation is so deceptively simple it's hard to believe that it can lower blood pressure, ease anxiety and depression, help with overcoming addictions, increase compassion, improve mental strength, reduce pain, extend life, and facilitate awakening. It is available to everyone regardless of religious orientation or economic position. Among my students have been practicing Catholics, Jews, and people who consider themselves spiritual but not affiliated with any religion. They have all incorporated meditation into their life while maintaining their faith or their world-view. This is because meditation is a practice, not a religion, and as such it does not require any given belief system. Nor does it require a high level of education or special circumstances. It is available to everyone whether they live in a mansion or in a jail, whether they have a PhD or have never finished high school, whether they identify as male, female or non-binary. Meditation is a great equalizer. *Anyone* can awaken to their true nature through daily practice. Sounds too good to be true? But it *is* true. History is rife with stories of people from different countries, different economic circumstances, different levels of education, different genders and different degrees of personal freedom who have awakened. This possibility belongs to you right now.

Meditation is extremely useful for parents and other caregivers. We who do so much for other people don't always take the time to focus on ourselves. When we meditate we pull in our energy, away from other people and tasks. It's a time to draw closer to ourselves, to enfold ourselves in warmth and remember who we are beyond what we do for others. Wrapping ourselves in a shawl and leaving our cares and worries behind, we enter a space where there is no need to fix or care for anything or anybody. Our body becomes a room of our own where we can retreat and enjoy a fresh perspective. Even after just 20 minutes we can re-enter the world refreshed and recharged.

There are many delights and levels of unfoldment in store for meditators, from physical and mental ease to a deeper understanding of the Universe and our place in it, confidence in our ability to deal with what life hands us, the skill to roll with the punches and to find deeper meaning and purpose in life. Through meditation we develop the ability to weave the dry straw of our life into gold. Starting with our own quiet practice of listening, we then carry that listening into daily life. As we experience more and more connections to everything and everyone around us, a deeper love of the world opens up. Our compassion grows effortlessly out of the realization that we are not alone, not separate, but connected to and a part of everything. Finally, through the equanimity developed during our sitting practice, we let go of the illusion that we can control life and we release into an even deeper freedom and order.

Through acts of nature or acts of humanity all material things and life circumstances can vanish at any time. The people and animals we love will come and go from our lives, we will age and our fortunes will increase and decrease. But meditation is always there to reconnect us with something real and deep and beautiful. Once you learn how to meditate it becomes your companion for life. No one can take it away from you. You can carry it with you out of a burning building and use it to rebuild your home. Even when our mind is foggy, meditation enables us to climb up the mountain past the fog into clarity. Through meditation we connect with our true nature, the part of us that is not dependent upon conditions.

It doesn't take a long time to start reaping the benefits of meditation. All it takes is some good instruction, commitment to the process, and the courage to try something new. It is a great benefit to have a group of people to meditate with but that is not always available. That is why it is so important to find ways to support home sitting practice.

Reading about meditation does very little. You don't become a good tennis player by simply watching people play tennis, or enjoy the fruits of a meal by watching a cooking show, and you don't reap the benefits of meditation by simply reading about it. The way to benefit from meditation is to create the space for practice, bolster courage and support, make a commitment, and follow through. In the following chapters we will explore some different ways to support home practice and some of the challenges and sights along the path.

Explore the benefits of meditation—decide for yourself if it is worth pursuing

WHAT IS MEDITATION?

It is a chilly winter morning in Vermont. The night before there was a slow steady snowfall which left the landscape powdery white with bare, brown tree branches lifting up to the sky. When opening the door, a snowdrift is pushed off to the side in a fluffy mound. My eyes are blinded by the purity of the white landscape. All is quiet. There is an icy still cocooned in a soundless sound. I can hear the silence. I feel connected to everything.

We can learn a lot about meditation from nature. In meditation we are like mountains and rivers. We go about our business without entertaining worry or judgment. Listening to the silence, we sink into a state of bare awareness. We just sit. A calm that is not dependent on circumstances settles in. We sit with the sound of ocean waves crashing on the shore or we sit with the sound of traffic and sirens and street noises. It's all connected—nothing is left out. We take a break from labeling some sounds as good and other sounds as bad and just listen to the symphony of the moment with alertness and curiosity.

Just sitting without doing anything is so simple we can barely grasp it. We spend our days going from one item on the to-do list to the next. We transfer that way of thinking onto meditation and think we need to be doing something, or not doing something, while meditating when in fact we just need to be present. Unlike most other activities in our life, meditation is not goal oriented. It requires a shift in consciousness from doing to *being* if we are to experience the benefits. But just being present can feel strange and uncomfortable to many of us. Since it feels odd to release control and just *be*, our mind comes up with all sorts of distractions to help us run away from the present moment as uninvited thoughts and feelings bubble up to the surface.

In this global age many meditation techniques are available through books and teachers; Transcendental Meditation, mindfulness meditation, Koan meditation, Tantric meditation, Tonglen, Shikentaza, Mahamudra, and Vipassana, to name just a few. There is a veritable smorgasbord of options. Each meditation technique has its strengths, and different techniques work best for different personalities at different times. What feels natural to you may not be the same as what feels natural to your friend, or even to you at a later date. I'd like to offer my understanding of what meditation is, behind the techniques, and give some basic meditation instruction. Hopefully this discussion will support whatever form of meditation you feel most at home with.

So, let's take a moment to break it down. Sitting practices are sometimes divided into two basic categories: contemplation and meditation. In Buddhism contemplation refers to practices that involve thinking and imagination such as visualization, where the mind is used to create images or feelings, or Lectio Divina, where the mind reflects on wisdom passed down through the written word. Contemplative practices are directive. We are guiding the mind in a chosen direction, such as towards love or letting go or wisdom. These techniques have valuable mental and spiritual effects, but bare bones meditation takes us in a different direction. Unlike contemplation, meditation is non-directive. In meditation we sit with things as they are without reflecting on anything. It is an exercise in letting go into the vastness of the present moment and listening to life as it is.

How many times have I heard people say, *I'm a bad meditator, I just can't concentrate and empty my mind.* But meditation isn't mind control. Thoughts continue to rise and fall just as the breath rises and falls. This is natural. Meditation does not require a peaceful or centered mind. We come to the pillow however we are and let everything be as it is. We may feel angry or agitated, sleepy, confused or crystal clear—it doesn't matter. Instead of thinking of meditation as stopping all thoughts, or thinking beautiful thoughts, we can think of it as presence, or listening, without attaching to the content of the thoughts, feelings and sensations. Rather than creating more suffering by trying to force the mind to go against its natural inclination to be active, we give our mind a break from judgment and control. We allow the mind to be totally free range and organic, creating the opposite of suffering: ease, peace, and awareness.

In silent illumination practice, also called shikantaza, mahamudra or just sitting, we let go of any scaffolding that has been holding up our sense of self. We just sit. With a straight spine and comfortable position, we feel our body, hear the sounds in the room, are aware of the coming and going of thoughts and feelings and let that be enough. No need to interact with the thoughts, feelings and sensations. Without the fuel of our attention they slowly fade away. We continue to sit. We may start with just 5 or 10 minutes and work up from there. As time goes on, or maybe right away for some, the freedom is palpable.

You are vast open space and your thoughts, sensations, and feelings are space junk flying through that space. Some days all we are doing during meditation is watching the junk fly in front of us and then dissolve. Through non-judgmental noticing a container is created that gives the thoughts and feelings freedom so they can settle down naturally. All manner of things fly through the mind then disappear into the nothingness from which they came. If there is no attachment or repulsion to the thoughts and feelings it's like watching a meteor shower—everything just comes and goes. That which is watching the meteor shower is who you are. After a while, thoughts and feelings settle down. They are still there but they are clearly flying through empty space.

Take a few moments to sit down and watch your thoughts and feelings without judgment

LETTING EVERYTHING BE AS IT IS

How do we relax into silence when there is so much going on inside our mind and body? Our body is chattering away about aches and pains, our mind is chattering away about lists, remembered conversations, past events and future fears or delights. Our mind is like a child wanting to do what it wants to do when it wants to do it while at the same time needing limits in order for it to feel safe and thrive. We are the parents of our own mind. If we are too punitive, too restrictive, our mind will rebel. If we are too loose our mind will do whatever it wants to do—whether it is for its highest good or not. Our ego will wiggle out of anything it deems uncomfortable or threatening. When we find that sweet spot between rigid and lax our mind knows that there is an adult in the room and can relax. Meditation is a perfect time and place to cultivate this balance.

Balance and self-kindness begin before we even sit down to meditate. When we create a structure for our sitting practice our mind has the opportunity to anticipate, and even look forward to, meditation. Our chosen time doesn't need to be first thing in the morning or right before bed or any other specific time. But it does make a difference if we create some sort of consistency in the time we sit, whatever that time might be. Staying with a regular time gives our mind the opportunity to prepare for meditation. Just like our child, our mind feels safest when there are parameters, not rigid arbitrary parameters but firm, strong, kind ones.

Once we have chosen a time and place for our practice, we can cultivate a comfortable sitting position. Before sitting down, it helps to stretch out a bit to prepare the body. While sitting still, discomfort we can ignore when the body is in motion becomes pronounced. Attending to the physical aspect of sitting, although not necessary, can be a great aid. When we're relaxed we can be more alert—like a cat stalking a mouse. Yoga postures and diet have been used for centuries to help meditators become comfortable with stillness.

Once our body is comfortable and our spine is erect the rest is up to personal preference—pillows, no pillows, a sofa, chair, or bench— whatever feels most supportive. It's important to take some time to discover the best sitting set up for your unique needs. From that place of comfort and acceptance, the body can then relax and release whatever is getting in the way of its natural state of ease. If you need to sneeze, sneeze, or, you can watch what it feels like in your body to want to sneeze and use that as a meditation object. Rigidity is not meditation. Meditation is presence—softly allowing everything to be as it is.

Some people sit with their eyes closed while others sit with their eyes open. Each way has its benefits. When the eyes are closed visual distractions are eliminated. When the eyes are open we develop the ability to be present even when there are visual distractions. It's useful to try it both ways—eyes open gazing at the ground a few feet in front of you or eyes closed. We want to give ourselves every opportunity to experience success, to look forward to our time in meditation. I like to wrap myself in a blanket when I meditate. It makes me feel contained and cozy. Cocooning myself in warmth signals that this is a time for nurturance, a time for turning within. I set a timer so that I'm free to sink into meditation knowing that the meditation will close with a bell after the designated period of time without my having to worry about time during meditation.

Once a sitting position is chosen, we can settle into our body with kindness towards whatever is found there. Sometimes aches and pains we can ignore while we're active zoom up front and center. Rather than resist any of these sensations we can turn toward them and meet them with curiosity. Where does the sensation start? Is it sharp or dull? Does it stay or does it come and go? By allowing the aches and pains to run their course rather than tightening up around them or trying to ignore them, the body receives the message that it is free to be just as it is. What is that sensation in my lower back? It feels like heat or hot impulses. What happens if I go deeper into the sensation rather than try to avoid it?

It seems counterintuitive to go towards what we perceive as pain. But, since pain is an inevitable aspect of the human experience there is great power in developing this skill. Turning towards pain is like a warrior turning around to face an enemy. It takes courage and imparts strength. While giving birth I turned towards the birthing pains and, although it was a wild ride for a while, I was eventually able to relax around the contractions. As the fear of pain slowly dissipated, tightness around each contraction diminished. I became less fearful and the pain quieted down. By the time the baby was born I was clear- exhausted, and blissful. We can experience the magic of turning toward less intense pain and watch it transform in the safe space of our daily meditation. That skill can then transfer to more challenging circumstances.

As arising thoughts and feelings are received with the same open acceptance that our body has just enjoyed, a deeper mental relaxation sets in. Rather than try to control what we are thinking or feeling we can watch it all arise and dissolve. The thoughts and feelings are like leaves falling from a tree. Whatever thought, feeling or sensation is strongest becomes our meditation object. When there is nothing grabbing our attention, we can anchor our attention in awareness of the in breath and the out breath, feeling the sensation of the breath at the nostrils or the abdomen. Intermittently we may be aware of sounds in the room, sensations in the body, thoughts and feelings that have run away with our attention, and anything else that stands out.

Anger, sadness, loneliness, elation, memories—all are free to arise and vanish in a welcoming atmosphere. Grounded in the understanding that thoughts and emotions are a natural part of being human, we receive, hear, and allow each one to share the same open space we just created for our body. It is easy to be seduced by interesting thoughts, but during meditation we are not concerned with the content of our thoughts. When we find ourselves sucked down a rabbit hole of a thought, feeling or sensation we gently bring ourselves back to the present moment. We are like Australian sheepdogs rounding up stray sheep and bringing them home. Our sheepdogs are our arsenal of techniques such as following the breath or labeling thoughts, feelings, and sensations. Without reprimand or discouragement the sheep dog brings the mind back to the present moment again and again.

Another word for meditation is listening. Dharma, or God, or life wisdom, is everywhere. While sitting in silence we become quiet enough to be aware of something bigger than our everyday concerns. We experience life directly, without interference from our thinking. Doors we didn't even know were there appear and open. Slowly, stillness sets in. We remember who we are beyond the broken heart, the painful body, and all the other things in our life that usually define us. For these few moments of meditation we are free! When the timer chimes and meditation is over it's lovely to take a moment to notice how we are feeling. The freedom touched on in meditation goes on to color our everyday life in wonderful and mysterious ways.

Find a place to sit comfortably, set a timer for however long feels right to you and watch your mind without any goal

RESISTANCE TO MEDITATION

Given that the practice of meditation asks so little of us—just a place to sit down and maybe a timer—yet gives us so much, you would think that everyone who discovers meditation would become lifelong practitioners. But…there is some small print. The practice requires the courage to sit down and look, without judgment, at all the thoughts and feelings whirling around in our mind, many of which we are desperately trying to avoid. All day long we distract ourselves with chores, electronic devices, food, work, conversations, and a myriad of other things. We create a sense of who we think we are by all the noise we are surrounded by. We are afraid if we stop…and be quiet… we will cease to exist. Pretty scary stuff! It's not that we can't find the time—even five minutes, to settle our mind. It's that there is an underlying fear of what we might hear if we stop for a moment and listen.

I understand this resistance. It has validity. Sitting down and observing what is going on in our mind and body is a courageous act. All day long we fend off fears, shame, and personal demons with our constant activity. Stopping, even for just five minutes, could give the demons time to rise up and….what? Eat us alive? Invalidate our existence? When they are unexamined, the fear and shame demons become a constant undercurrent in our lives. In fact, they run our lives. It's easier to just give in to them than turn around and face them. In the meantime they inflict untold damage to our sense of well- being, our family, and our world.

Another reason meditation can feel threatening is because it challenges us to loosen our grip on control. In our daily life we need to be on top of work assignments, paying bills, seeing to our children's education, health care and hundreds of other very real concerns. When we meditate we are asked to let go of control. Even letting go of control for only 20 minutes can feel very strange, even dangerous. If we stop holding up the world, who will make sure it doesn't fall in a heap? So, even though we know that meditation will make our lives infinitely better, deep down inside we're not sure the benefits are worth facing the ensuing existential crisis. We may not be aware of this dynamic but we feel the hot breath of a looming threat so we sabotage our practice.

The Buddha noticed five basic ways the mind distracts itself from just sitting: sensory desire, irritation, sleepiness, restlessness and doubt. Although we know meditation will help us in so many ways our mind employs these five strategies to avoid sitting. We feel we are too tired to meditate or just can't sit still due to prickly feelings of irritation, or think there is something more pleasant, or more urgent, to do than sitting in silence. We have our doubts that sitting in silence will even be of any value. We become restless and anesthetize ourselves with television, phones, activities, intoxicants, other people, and work. We convince ourselves that we are too busy, too tired, too sick, our house is too noisy—yadda, yadda, yadda. The ego is brilliant at getting us out of things it doesn't want us to do.

While teaching meditation to moms for over 20 years, I've witnessed this conflict between a desire to meditate and resistance to taking the time to meditate play out in person after person. In monasteries meditators are supported to continue meditating through the hindrances by having designated times set up for sitting together. It's much easier to continue to sit in silence when there is community support. But those of us who work and keep a home usually have no such group to sit with at regular times. We have to rely on ourselves to get to the pillow and stay seated until the bell rings. This is not a problem for highly disciplined people. But for the rest of us, creating a consistent meditation practice may seem easy at first glance but in reality, it is a steep climb. Maintaining a sitting practice is truly a heroic act.

Once we decide that meditation will be of benefit to us, how do we overcome our resistance and give ourselves the support we need to meditate at home? Because resistance can be so strong, we need to employ every form of support we can muster up.

Take a moment to reflect on how you resist meditation

SUPPORTING THE PRACTICE

There are those who set up a meditation habit and stick with it regardless of what their day entails. Daily meditation becomes as basic as brushing their teeth. Then there are others—and I include myself in this group—who find it challenging to stick to a schedule. We come up with all sorts of valid excuses to neglect what we know is good for us—*I don't feel well, my family life is too demanding right now, and* (fill in the blank). Even sitting for just five minutes seems undoable. There is nothing wrong with you, it's natural to feel resistence. I've been meditating for over 50 years and still need support for daily practice. If an old Dharma nerd like me falters from consistent practice then someone new to meditation, someone who hasn't yet tasted the fruits of the practice, is dealing with resistance, and has a demanding work and family life, certainly needs as much support as they can get. Over the years I've discovered three classic ways cultures throughout the world support meditation practice; ritual, consistency, and community.

The first form of support is ritual. Although ritual is often associated with religion, it need not be. Rituals are poems. They are visual metaphors for unseen qualities, such as hope, beauty, warmth, kindness, and connectivity. Through the poetic beauty of ritual we are reminded to experience a deeper sense of purpose in our life. Creating ritual around our sitting practice elevates the practice and reminds us that what we are using our valuable time for has depth and importance. Ritual creates awareness of the beauty in things we take for granted and encourages us to enjoy the moment.

Spiritual systems throughout the world employ various rituals to inspire awareness. One of the most universal and time-tested rituals is the creation of an altar. Altars have been created all over the world for ages to evoke a more interior reality. When traveling through

Myanmar every home I visited had an altar. In one of the homes a full half of the small interior space was set up as a home altar. It was impressive how this family that had so little space devoted half of it to their spiritual practice.

For the last couple of decades I've had the good fortune to be a friend on the path to many moms through the *Hearth Foundation*. In *Hearth*'s first set of classes we created personal altars designed to support our home meditation practice. The process we use to create a home altar is simple:

1. During the first week we designate a place in our home for meditation, much like a cat finds a special cozy spot to curl up in.

2. Once we've found our spot, a little altar—a bench, a table, a window sill or any other flat space where we can place the rest of the building blocks—is created within our chosen spot.

3. Then we find a picture or object that reminds us of our spiritual aspirations, such as a Buddha statue, a picture of Mother Teresa or Mary, a statue of Kwan Yin, or a picture of our personal teacher. This inspiration is placed on the altar.

4. Then we find some sort of light, such as a candle or lamp, and set it on the altar to inspire warmth and insight in our practice.

5. We take a walk with our kids, or on our own, to find flowers, stones, and other natural objects to build an arrangement for our altar that will remind us of our connection to the natural world.

6. Finally, incense, a scented candle, or an essential oil diffuser is added to inspire us to be present when we breathe. To remember the beauty in life.

Once the space for home meditation has been created, there are some other simple ways to support daily practice. One way is to choose how long we want to sit and set a timer. Some start with five minutes and work up to a half hour or maybe 20 minutes. When starting, keep it short and sweet. It is more important to establish a habit than to meditate for a long time. After a week or two of consistent sitting for short sessions you may want to increase your amount of sitting time. Some people enjoy long practice periods, others find they do best with 20 or 30 minutes. Once, when a student was bragging about how long he could sit, his teacher, Ajhan Chah, commented that a chicken sits on an egg all day. The main thing is not how long you sit but how present you are when you're sitting. Better to start slowly and develop a love for meditation.

The second time tested way to support meditation practice is developing some consistency. What time of the day do you prefer to sit? Many people like to sit in the early morning before the family awakens and before their busy day begins. There is a special magic in the air before the world starts stirring. It's quiet. Life is a blank slate. When we sit in the morning, we begin the day centered and bring that quality to our waking family and morning activities. But not everyone is able, or inclined, to sit first thing in the morning, and it's not necessary to pick this time. Some of the moms I worked with like to sit before or after work or in the afternoon when their children are in school. Others like to sit in the evening when the family is home. This can be a sweet way to share the practice with our family. Each family is different and has different needs. Whatever works best for your life, it helps to pick a consistent time to meditate. Consistency is an essential part of building any habit.

The creation of ritual and consistency are two important elements of a home sitting practice, and as long as my students were with the group this was enough to bring them to the meditation pillow for daily sitting. They enjoyed the process of creating an altar and they enjoyed their meditation. But I've noticed over the years that once the group disbanded, the practice usually dissolved as well. Even with a strong desire to meditate, knowledge about how to meditate and a designated place to sit, there is still a need for consistent support and inspiration in order to maintain a vibrant practice. It seems there is no getting around this issue of community. Even the monk in a cave has the support of friends on the path. Even the teacher needs her students. We need each other and we need the support of other dedicated practitioners, or teachers, to keep us inspired.

Once, when asked if sangha, or community of like-minded practitioners, was part of the path the Buddha replied that spiritual community is not part of the path—it *is* the path. In our individualistic modern culture, we think we have to go it alone. Many of us are phobic about any group that smacks of spirituality or religion. Some of us feel that we should be above needing other people to support us. But if we isolate in our practice we do not go as far as quickly and we are liable to get stuck down the many dark alleys of our mind. We are social animals and, although meditation is an interior process, we are awakening together.

Companionship on the path is the secret glue that keeps the simple practice of meditation vibrant and alive. Although we enter our own private world in meditation we are not alone. It's essential that we remember that we're in this together. Finding others to sit with, and possibly a teacher or spiritual friend who can offer guidance, even just once a week, once a month, or even once a year, gives our practice a stronger foundation. It ties our practice to the rest of the world and reminds us that we are not out there all alone, we are part of something bigger.

Take some time to find a place in your home for practice. Choose a time of day and how long to sit, set up a small altar and create beauty around your practice. Find others, or at least one other person—to sit with.

MEDITATION SUPPORT
FOR FUZZY BRAINS

We all go through times when, even if our practice is strong, we just can't seem to focus. Maybe we're really angry or grieving or hung over or have some sort of allergies or medical condition, or maybe we're just not at the top of our game. Fear not, intrepid meditator, help is on the way! Because of medical conditions, I've spent a lot of time dealing with mental fog and have become somewhat of an expert at operating heavy mental machinery in the midst of a dense haze.

Meditation is often associated with concentration, something that is difficult to do with a fuzzy brain. But the word *concentration* is unfortunate. It conjures up images of forced control and trying to make something happen. Trying to force the mind is counterproductive, like telling someone to "just relax." As is the case with teenagers, forcing is the least skillful, least effective tactic. Try as we may, we can't control our way into a clear, open mind or muscle our way into a state of ease. We need to respect where the mind is at and meet it there. Although we can't control, we can influence. Rather than berate our mind for its rebellion, if we listen to its needs without judgment it's much more receptive to opening up for us.

Meditation is listening, and it is just as possible to listen to a foggy brain as it is to listen to a clear brain. On a foggy day we can't see the blue of the sky or feel the warmth of the sun. But they are still there and, although we can't see the sky, we can look at the fog that is in the sky. The fog in our mind is just dispersed clouds drifting through our sky. When we focus on the sky that the fog drifts through we turn the tables on the situation and suddenly we are lucid in meditation. This becomes easier over time as we develop a stronger relationship with the sky—the ground that lies underneath the constant thoughts, feelings, sensations and fog. But until we become established in this ground there are a few techniques that I've found helpful when struggling to meditate.

Sometimes, when I am too restless to meditate, I burn off the jagged energy by walking quickly with awareness. Fast walking is particularly helpful during times of anger or depression, each of which have physical manifestations. Anger brings with it a prickly restlessness. Quick walking helps release the jumpy body sensations and brings awareness back to the moment. Quick walking during times of dullness and ennui can help awaken our body from its withdrawal. Slowly we come back to life.

There are also yoga positions that help settle the mind and bring ease to the body. Over many centuries, yogis have developed wisdom about eating and movement, some of it designed to help the body become lighter and more receptive during meditation. Monastics in other traditions have also discovered how food and drink affect meditation. Just as when we eat sugar we feel a burst of energy and then a steep decline, when we eat foods that provide the body with sustained energy we are more apt to feel centered and meditation is easier. Zen monks even developed the use of green tea in order to help them focus during long meditation sessions. If our body is struggling it is difficult to develop a calm mind. It can be done but why not give ourselves all the support possible.

Once we sit down to meditate there are a number of techniques that help center a foggy brain. When I was studying with my first teacher, Anagarika Dhammadinna, she had me mentally touch points on my body with my imagination while sitting cross-legged in meditation to help ground my energy. Instead of counting breaths or labeling thoughts, feelings and sensations, she had me pick four points where my body was touching the ground and place awareness on them one at a time; left butt cheek, right knee, right butt cheek, left knee. Going from right to left across the body tethered me to the pillow I was sitting on. Awareness of sensation at each point required focus. This was the added focus I needed for my wild, jagged ADD addled mind.

We can also anchor ourselves during foggy times by counting breaths. Early on in his career teaching meditation to Westerners, Chogyam Trungpa had his students just sit in the vastness without much technique. This approach to meditation is called mahamudra in Tibetan Buddhism and shikantaza in Japanese Zen. He eventually realized that his students were having a hard time becoming grounded with this bare bones approach so he added breath focus. As long as we are alive the breath is always there, which makes it a perfect, ever-present meditation object. There are a number of different ways to employ the breath for meditation. The Zen way is to count 10 breaths and, if you are somehow able to get to 10 without having your mind wander off, go back to one again. You can also focus on the breath at your nostrils, feeling the cool air as you inhale and the warm air as you exhale.

Another tool to help anchor ourselves in the present moment is Vipassana meditation. In Vipassana, when we feel the breath at the nostril or abdomen, we label this as "breathing, breathing, breathing." Vipassana anchors us in the moment by having us label each thought, feeling, and sensation as they arise to bring ourselves back to the moment. Whatever is strongest in our awareness becomes the meditation object. For instance, we are sitting and start thinking about an item on our to-do list. As soon as we notice we've left the present moment we take note of the thought and say inwardly "thinking, thinking, thinking." and return to our breath. The content of the thought doesn't matter. What matters is noticing that we have flown off on a reverie and are now returning to the present moment. The same is the case with emotions and physical sensations. As soon as we notice that we've left the present moment we use awareness of the distraction to bring ourselves back to what is happening right now. What is so great about this technique is that it omits nothing. Whatever is foremost in our awareness becomes our meditation object—no holds barred. That which pulls us out of presence is used to return us to presence.

There are times we need more support and times when meditation feels easy. It's good to be ready with different strategies to support ourselves through whatever we are experiencing. It's like having a first aid kit in the house. We don't need bandages every day but we are grateful to have them there when we scrap our knees. When we feel well, we don't even think about our first aid kit, but when we're sick, we are so glad it is there.

Have strategies in place for times when you need more support

THE FRUITS OF MEDITATION

I'm sitting outside on the deck under the shade of an old faded umbrella. On a little glass table beside me sits an earthenware teapot filled to the brim with sweet oolong tea. The deck is surrounded by all shades of green, multiple shapes of leaves and weeds, roses, reds, oranges, corals, violets, rose of Sharon bushes, basil, and fruit trees opening their arms to the sky in a full summer embrace. There's a slight breeze through the wooden clackers. Once in a while a green unripe apple falls off the tree sounding like a drum on the deck. My granddaughter, Nai'a, plays in the sandbox as I talk with a friend on the phone and drink tea.

When I was a new mom I felt the weight of immense responsibility. I had to feed and clothe and teach this precious little person, pay bills, swim the treacherous seas of romantic and family relationships, and try to get enough sleep. This was made more challenging by a painful divorce, becoming a single parent, and Chronic Fatigue Syndrome. While going through my private heavens and hells I was able to remain buoyant and keep my head above water as wave after wave crashed down on me. The rock I clung to was my spiritual practice. I honestly don't know where I'd be now without the support of meditation and spiritual inquiry.

Now, as a grandma who has had modest insight into how all things are interconnected, I watch my moods, fatigue, pressures, highs and lows, always with the question "What is it that feels moody, tired, stressed, high, low?" I look and look but there's nothing there. All I can find is that place I visit while in meditation. Everything arises and fades into that...what? Vastness? I don't know what it is. The constant thread tying together all the sensations and thoughts that continually arise and fade away is the emptiness, for lack of a better word, in which they exist. Feelings, sights, sounds, plans, worries, desires all swimming in rich, full, sparkling emptiness.

My life is not perfect, I have plenty of challenges, but there is an underlying bliss, a bliss that is not dependent on shifting moods, bodily complaints, how much money I have, or don't have, how my body feels, or what other people think of me. This confidence is the fruit of a lifetime of meditation and spiritual practice, one of the priceless gifts of the Dharma. We don't have to wait until our families are out of the house or until our life has settled down to know the fruits of meditation. We can know them in the midst of crying babies, challenging teenagers, and the ever-shifting sands of our richly embroidered lives.

How can I share this beautiful practice with you? How can busy homemakers blend absolute emptiness with the relativity of everyday responsibilities? How can they remember that everything is interconnected and meaningful even when they are tired and the baby is crying or the teenager is saying "I hate you"? How can they remember a moment of freedom, when their attention was pure and they were not at war with things the way they are? When awareness is brought into feelings like fatigue or sadness the feeling becomes just another passing sensation. The sensation dissolves into the fullness of the moment.

Nai'a comes crying into my arms. The sound of the dog barking in the distance joins the symphony of the wooden clacker, the drum beat of the apples, the rustling tree, and Nai'a's diminishing weeping. We sit together, perfectly there, emptiness present in the love, emptiness present in the tears, her warm breath on my shoulder. Her tears wind down and we just sit together, cuddle, and listen to the back yard. This is a good life.

Walking

After sitting we stand up and walk back into our lives. How do we walk our renewed presence into our home, family life, work and daily activities?

This section is about bringing the awareness we are cultivating during meditation into the hundreds of activities we perform each day. How do we enjoy our life just the way it is without resistance?

So, the first principle of the Zen cook is that we already have everything we need. If we look closely at our lives, we will find that we have all the ingredients we need to prepare the supreme meal. At every moment, we simply take the ingredients at hand and make the best meal we can. It doesn't matter how little we have. The Zen cook just looks at what is available and starts with that.

Bernard Glassman Roshi,
from Instructions to the Cook

FINDING THE JOY WHERE WE ARE

Upon seeing the morning star the Buddha exclaimed, "How wonderful! How wonderful! Everything is enlightened. All beings and all things are enlightened just as they are".

Koan variation from *Keizan, Transmission of the lamp*

Each life has its unique challenges and callings. Some are called to make a difference in the world through politics, business, and other endeavors outside the home; some are called to make a difference inside the home; and other lives are combinations of infinite variety. But the end game is the same—to live a full, rich life and, hopefully, to make the world a better place for our having been here. This is what most of us want, regardless of age, position, education, political leanings, or degree of wealth.

There are few places one can find a simple path to a rich life better illuminated than in the work of Brother Lawrence, a 17th century Parisian Catholic monk. At the age of 18 Brother Lawrence had an awakening. While looking at a bare tree in winter he realized that this same tree, through the grace of God, will be filled with green leaves and fruit without any outside effort. This awakening turned Brother Lawrence towards God and led him to a new life as a Carmelite monk. His awakening brings to mind expressions of Zen awakenings, such as Lingyun Zhiqin's peach blossom realization:

> *For thirty years I have looked for a sword.*
> *Many times leaves fell, new ones sprouted.*
> *One glimpse of peach blossoms,*
> *Now no more doubts—*
> *Just this.*

Brother Lawrence was born poor, uneducated, and uninterested in espousing theories or debating fine points. Because he was uneducated, when he became a monk he was given the task of tending the monastery kitchen. As he did his chores, love of God fueled devout attention to each task. His prayer was:

Lord of all pots and pans and things
Make me a saint by getting meals
And washing up the plates.

This little verse offers a glimpse into how practicing the presence might look for the homemaker. There is not a lot written about the simple practice of fully entering the moment in daily life, perhaps because the practitioners of this homey spiritual artform are not as interested in leaving marks as are their more intellectual brothers and sisters. But we can discover footprints in the poetry and stories left behind from various traditions.

17th century Europe was a time filled with power struggles, wars, debts, and perpetual unrest—a tumultuous time like our own. It was in this challenging climate that Brother Lawrence led his simple life of continually turning towards God in all activities. He did not let chronic pain from a disability he endured while young deter him. He did not let what he deemed unpleasant tasks, such as traveling to negotiate and collect wine for the monastery, deter him. He continued to practice through the pleasant and the unpleasant.

Some might call Brother Lawrence's practice mindfulness. But his practice had a very different texture than our 21st century Western version of mindfulness. As opposed to raw mindfulness, Brother Lawrence's mindfulness was infused with joy and awe and a sense of something greater than himself. He felt that "… *in this conversation with God we are also employed in praising, adoring, and loving Him incessantly, for his infinite goodness and perfection."*

Eastern spiritual practices, upon entering the West's mainstream, met a highly materialistic culture. Mindfulness practice became a mental exercise to deal with physical and emotional pain and a method to encourage moment-to-moment awareness to better our lives. This interpretation of mindfulness practice has real value, both physical and psychological, but is often devoid of the unpredictable mystical elements of love, gratitude, surrender, and reverence. The danger of leaving the mystery out of mindfulness practice is that the practice can devolve into an attempt to control or run away from our life rather than surrendering to the unfoldment of our life as it is and finding joy therein.

In order for our happiness to not be dependent upon conditions we need to ballast our lives to something greater than the changing winds that sweep us here and there. For Brother Lawrence that ballast was God. How do we—the sons and daughters of a materialistic culture—surrender, trust, and open our hearts if we are unable to summon up a heartfelt belief in some force higher than ourselves?

Although the concept of God is a classic and powerful way to connect with the mystery, and has been of great value to mystics throughout the ages, our embrace of the mystical doesn't need to be tied to that word or, for that matter, to religion. Thankfully, the mystical does not depend on religion, or religious terminology, for its expression. The mystery is ubiquitous. Religion at its best is a culture's container for the truth that is everywhere and in everything. This truth resides in the question *who am I?* It resides in the fact that we are alive, thinking, and communicating beings. It resides in the mystery of what happens when we die and how we were born into this life, this family, this culture. It resides in the miracle that this planet has developed an abundance of life forms, that we are made of stardust, that realizations can leave us in a state of awe and connect us with all other life forms.

As Dogen Zenji, the great teacher who brought Soto Zen to Japan in the 13th century wrote,

> *Everything—blooming flowers, wild grasses, mountains, oceans, land, rivers, is the body and spirit of original Buddha mind. This original mind is a chair, a bamboo, or a tree.*

Where we were born, the family we were born into, how we will die, and how each small and large detail between birth and death comes to be, are mysteries. In our practice we let go into the mystery that resides in each moment and in each blade of grass. Like the blade of grass, we are simultaneously an insignificant and an essential aspect of the whole.

The essence of everyday practice is to see the miracle in everything we do and everything we come into contact with, whether we are washing dishes, making love, filling out paperwork or reading to a child. The challenge is to remember that life is a gift: to not take our unique and essential life for granted, to trust its unfoldment, and remember that there is wisdom at work that is larger than we can possibly comprehend and that everything we see, hear, smell, touch, and taste is an aspect of God or original Buddha nature. When we bring this sense of awe and surrender into our daily mindfulness practice, we can begin to see the miracle in each dirty dish.

Find your way into a sense of awe within the mundane

WALKING

To find the universal elements enough, to find the air and the water exhilarating, to be refreshed by a morning walk or an evening saunter, to be thrilled by the stars at night, to be elated over a bird's nest or a wildflower in spring — these are some of the rewards of the simple life.

John Burroughs

Walking in the early morning when there is still a chill in the air left over from the night before, everything feels fresh with possibility. I walk over damp, musky leaves, past the peeling bark of eucalyptus trees, past grape vines in straight rows moving towards the horizon, ubiquitous blackberry bushes covered with red and purple fruit and blue misty mountains in the background. The delicious air on my cheeks like ice cream, the fog clinging to the hills and the caw of the crow never fail to put me in a state of wonder. Henry David Thoreau wrote,

An early morning walk is a blessing for the whole day.

As wonderfully pastoral as the Sonoma countryside is, I've experienced the same wonder while walking in urban Los Angeles past shop windows filled with the inventions of many hands, the smell of tortillas cooking in food trucks, sidewalks cracked in jagged patterns with intrepid little plants making their way up to the sun, newsstands displaying a collage of colors, and people walking briskly. A walk in the city is filled with the miracle of being human—how infinitely inventive we are! Having a body that sees, smells, hears and feels is just as poignant in the city as it is in the country. It doesn't matter where we're walking, when we're unconditionally present we are saturated with the mystery of life all around us.

Buddhist practice includes bringing the unconditional awareness touched on while sitting into our walking. The first walking meditation I learned was vipassana. In the beginning it seemed odd—people walking back and forth slowly like zombies. But while trying it out I discovered that moving slowly makes it possible to sink more deeply into the moment. Having less to respond to makes awareness in the moment easier. In vipassana walking meditation we continually bring awareness back to the body much the same way we bring awareness back to the breath while sitting. Our awareness is present with the foot as it lifts, moves forward than touches the ground. We feel the intention to move and we feel the body as it travels through cool, warm or neutral spaces. While labeling each movement during deep meditation we focus on the minute movements of the mind and body. Walking meditation can be as precise as noticing all the details of each movement but can also be as general as being aware of moving through space.

There are many delightful ways to walk- walking with dogs, walking with children, walking with friends. A walk is a wonderful thing to share. But the experience of walking meditation is different than an amble with friends or walking while talking on the phone or listening to podcasts or music. Just as we wouldn't talk with a friend while meditating on our pillow, walking meditation asks us to let go of distractions and really experience our surroundings. As we walk we let go of each thought and feeling as it arises and return to awareness of the present moment; to our feet on the ground, the air, the smells. We become aware of sights and sounds without getting lost in them. Our skin feels the air, our limbs move through space, we smell and hear without attaching to, or recoiling from, anything. We continue to move through each moment—one after the other. Walking with awareness is as simple as just being where we are. We ask the question, who walks? As we travel on, there are no sights, only awareness of seeing—no sounds, only awareness hearing.

Everywhere we walk we encounter different sights and sounds and smells- it is all alive! In the city there are human imprints on the environment; graffiti, flowers planted in boxes, architecture, and the smells of perfume, cooking and urine. Can we set aside judgment when we experience smells that don't appeal to us and see them as part of the numinous whole? Can we enjoy the smell of jasmine without becoming attached to it? Walking on the beach there is the sound of the waves, the sound of children playing and dogs barking and cool, salty air. Can we put aside attachment to that which appeals to us and revulsion to that which we find distasteful and see everything as alive? When we approach whatever we encounter with choiceless awareness we open up to the richness and endless variety of life. The clarity we experience while walking with presence makes everything new, everything interesting. Everyday life becomes an adventure.

Take a walk by yourself. Put away all devices and experience yourself as part of the community. Feel the air, let the sights and smells come and go. Keep bringing yourself back to the present moment.

GATHA MEDITATION

In preparation for our journey through meditation verses, three thin volumes sit by my side. One is a translation of the *Dhammapada* that my mother helped make more accessible to a Western audience, one is a sliver of a book by Thich Nhat Hanh entitled *Present Moment, Wonderful Moment,* and the third is a book by Robert Aitken Roshi called *The Dragon Who Never Sleeps.*

Gatha is a Sanskrit term meaning verse or hymn. In classical Buddhist literature the word gatha is used to designate the versified portion of the sutras, or teaching stories. Verse and meditation have been intimately linked together since the beginning of religious thought. The use of verse as a carrier of wisdom is not only found in Buddhism but also in other religions throughout the world. The Torah, the Psalms, the Bible, and the Koran are just a few examples of illuminated words that contain an experience of the awakened mind. Gathas are equally as useful for beginners as they are for advanced practitioners. Part poetry, part affirmation, part practice instruction, gathas have the ability to cover a vast territory in a short amount of time. They are direct, bite size and incisive, offering a pocket practice we can carry anywhere and pull out at any time.

When we encounter just the right words, a door to a more expansive reality opens up before us. We can enter there. The words may be different for different cultures, different ages, and different personalities, but their effects are the same. When we meet these words, the spiritual world becomes not simply beautiful thoughts, but a very real experience of the numinous. Gathas have the power to open our inner eyes to new ways of seeing. They infuse us with the joy and depth that is available regardless of the circumstances we find ourselves in.

Looking at these slender little books before me—almost pamphlets really—it's clear that an inquiry into gathas is not going to be about research or scholarship. Since gathas are art forms we can't think our way through them. We need to feel and experience a gatha. The experience is a dance between our awareness and the present moment. The way into a gatha is through our own flesh-and-blood life—the dishes being washed, the snarky thought, the food being eaten, the pain in our heart—combined with openness to experiencing life in a fresh way. Here are a few gathas:

> *When I feel I haven't got time,*
> *I vow with all beings*
> *To light incense and, making my bows,*
> *Touch the place of no time.*
> Robert Aitken, Roshi

> *Entering the meditation room,*
> *I see my true mind.*
> *I vow that once I sit down,*
> *All disturbances will stop.*
> Thich Nhat Hanh

> *The wise man,*
> *By vigor, mindfulness, restraint, and self-control,*
> *Creates for himself an island*
> *Which no flood can submerge.*
> The *Dhammapada*

Although the above gathas deal directly with meditation, no situation is too small or too large for a gatha:

> *When the traffic is bumper to bumper*
> *I vow with all beings*
> *To move when the world starts moving*

And rest when it pauses again.
Robert Aitken, Roshi

May I cut you, little flower,
Gift of Earth and sky?
Thank you, dear bodhisattva,
For making life beautiful.
Thich Nhat Hanh

And the gatha we already visited:

Lord of all pots and pans and things…
Make me a saint by getting meals
And washing up the plates.
Brother Lawrence

Each of these gathas illuminate everyday life. Can you hear how different the voices of Aitken Roshi, the *Dhammapada*, Brother Lawrence, and Thich Nhat Hanh are? Each verse navigates the depths, yet each psyche is unique. Your awakening does not look like my awakening or Aitken Roshi's awakening or Thich Nhat Hanh's awakening, even though we inevitably touch the same basic truths. This is the case with the world's great religions and mystical systems. Each authentic system dives deep into the heart of the matter and brings up its treasures, conveying the depths to those of us living on the surface by using different languages and imagery for different cultures.

The challenges you encounter each day are different from the challenges I encounter. Because of this we may be attracted to different gathas. A gatha about ox herding is not so relevant to today's city dweller. A gatha about waiting in traffic is not so relevant to someone who doesn't drive. Allusions to plants and seasons appeal to some, allusions to graffiti and bus stations to others. Images and language evoke different things to different people given their life experiences. For this reason we need to continue creating new poems, new literature, and new gathas. They are living art forms.

We have all had some encounter with the deep wisdom at our core. A gatha is designed to remind us of who we are and help us tap into that depth of wisdom since we are all prone to forget. Both beginners and seasoned practitioners need to be reminded of the bigger picture over and over, regardless of how long we've been on this spiritual awakening journey. A gatha brings us there.

We can use gathas created by others who inspire us or we can create new gathas uniquely suited to our life. Nobody knows the best language to use or what situations we encounter daily better than ourselves. With a little support we can learn how to write our own gathas from that deep, still place within, the place we touch in meditation. Using language that is meaningful to us, our homemade gathas will touch our hearts powerfully and directly. They remind us of who we really are throughout the unique particulars of our day.

Find or create a small verse to bring out during a time you find challenging

ATTENTION IS LOVE

When we pay attention to a sprout in the garden, we notice when it needs water, when it needs pruning or fertilizing, when it needs extra protection from the elements. Since we are present with it, we can observe its condition and minister to its needs. The little sprout thrives. This holds true for all other elements in our life. What we pay attention to thrives—whether it is a relationship, our family, a fear, or a pursuit. Regardless of what we're born into, our age, how much money we have, where we live, or any other aspect of life we are experiencing, we all possess the power to make things grow by giving them our unconditional attention.

When we pay attention to the people around us we see them more clearly, enabling us to support and enrich their lives in ways that are meaningful. Giving this sort of attention to our friends and family is simple but can be challenging in our electronic age. Being in the same room as someone isn't the same as *being* with them. Even if our body is present our attention may be far away. A friend told me that his mother used to spend hours talking on the phone in the kitchen. This was back in the 50s when phones were attached to cords on kitchen walls. His mother was physically present a lot of the time but he still felt lonely. I see moms walking with their kids in the park and talking on cell phones while the child looks around for someone to connect with. The mother's attention is on whoever is on the other end of the line, not on her child. I see people walking in nature on a beautiful day plugged into their devices. They are not smelling the pine needles or seeing the mushrooms hiding behind a log. How many important and delightful moments are we missing by not being present?

When we pay attention to the land we notice the beauty of this improbable planet. While consciously walking in nature we become intimate with the birds, insects, plants, changing winds, and the elements. We sit on the warm sand at the beach and experience the sea's vastness. We watch a purple crocus pop up through the snow and witness the power of the life force. We learn to love, really love, this planet, by walking on its body consciously. If we do not spend time walking its body with awareness we're more apt to take it for granted. Our attention is elsewhere so it doesn't register when the winds are changing, when there is a different smell in the air, when the land is thirsty. When we hear the crows and notice a little yellow dandelion bravely pushing up through the concrete we learn to respect the life force in all its myriad forms.

Just as we express love for our family and our planet by giving them our unconditional attention, we express love for ourselves by listening and being present with our body just as it is. Women in our culture have been taught to pay critical, conditional attention to their bodies. We've been trained to look in the mirror and meticulously scan ourselves for flaws, to try and figure out how to make our body more appealing. We inject poison into our faces, undergo surgeries, and subject ourselves to rigorous diets in order to make ourselves more appealing. Adornment and beauty are universal expressions of joy, but when we torture ourselves over our looks, beautification becomes an act of self-loathing and looking in the mirror becomes an act of self-cruelty.

It is a miracle to have been born, to be reading these words. We honor this miracle when we pay loving attention to our body. Taking care of ourselves becomes even more vital when we are running a home and raising children. Caregivers tend to put everyone's needs before their own and often end up depleted. If we don't take care of ourselves our energy wanes. Then more and more things start falling through the cracks. When we take care of our own mind and body we reap the benefits of well-being while at the same time teaching our children how to take loving care of themselves by our example.

The light of our attention is like the sun to a plant. The sun warms and feeds the young plant and the plant takes energy from the sun converting it into more life. If we keep our attention on the darkness in the world, darkness becomes our worldview. If we put our attention on creative solutions the world becomes alive with possibility. It is attention with love that makes a house a home and attention with love that makes a child, a garden, our community, our love life, our own body and our spiritual life, thrive.

Unplug and pay unconditional attention to the things and people in your life

HOME AWAKENING

When I slid open the drawer to put a new pair of socks inside I encountered a mess of old, threadbare, sometimes unmatched, socks. Dumping the sock drawer out on the bed, I proceeded to sort out the still-useful from the—come on…when are you ever going to need one pink sock? After sorting, eliminating, and refolding, the sock drawer became more useful, even, dare I say, beautiful? When I open the sock drawer now it reminds me of a choice I made to be more aware. This sock drawer realization started a chain reaction that carried on for weeks. From socks I went to blouses, to T-shirts, to pants, to dresses, to the refrigerator, to the bookshelf, and beyond.

Most of us have our own versions of the sock drawer—the junk drawer, the hall closet, the attic, and often there are multiple areas in our home where we mindlessly store things. Since a home is alive, it is always falling apart and coming back together, getting messed up and recovering. Messiness is part of life and a beautiful home is not necessarily a perfect home. Our unfoldment is also messy and imperfect and beautiful. Like our home, our consciousness is in a constant state of becoming, falling apart, and settling. The places where we live reflect our ever-changing, imperfect states of mind.

We can learn a lot about ourselves by being aware in our environment. We can observe our home the same way we observe our mind in meditation. Is our home cluttered with redundant objects? Is it dependent on the approval of others? Do we feel free to express ourselves creatively in our home? Does our home nourish and embrace us when we walk through the door? Like MRIs for the body, our home shows us the inner workings of our deepest thoughts and feelings, an echo chamber where our inner self is made manifest and amplified. We share these echo chambers with our family who are intimately affected by the environment we create. Armed with this knowledge we can choose to develop environments that nurture us and our family and amplify that nurturance out into the world.

There is so much ingenuity that went into creating the walls that protect us, so much thought that went into the items that make our lives easier. With respect and appreciation for toilets, washing machines, ovens, and other household items we fix the ones that need fixing and let go of the ones that no longer serve us. This practice extends to everyday chores. With awareness we can approach dish washing, vacuuming, chopping vegetables, and boiling noodles with gratitude for the dishes that hold our sustenance, for the water that keeps us alive, for the ability to touch the smooth edges of the plate, and smell the lemon. We extend gratitude to the floors, the tables, the beds, and the chairs. It doesn't matter if a chair is plastic or an expensive chaise lounge. The chair enables us to sit and rest. Our awareness practice helps us fully enjoy the support that our chair, our bed, and our couch offer us.

There is much to be grateful for if we have shelter, whether it is big or small, owned or rented, in the city, the country, or the suburbs. I met a woman who lives in a trailer park in a run-down part of town. When you drive up to her trailer you're met by a garden that has been lovingly tended and teems with life. Her home and garden sit like a jewel set in aged metal. She brings joy and hope into that run-down neighborhood by the beauty of her home and garden.

As the awareness we touch on during meditation develops, we naturally bring that heightened awareness into our home. Our home becomes an extension of our practice. It is no longer a showplace designed to impress others or a place we carelessly retreat to. It is a place where we accept ourselves with all our imperfections, a safe incubator for awakening. Our home expresses and honors who we are and what we love. When we create beauty in our home—our own unique definition of beauty—we nourish our practice of awareness and we nourish our family and friends. A beautiful home is a powerful blessing and source of healing for all who enter.

We have the opportunity to actively engage in creativity and love every day in small and large ways as we tend our home. Our home is where we heal, where we replenish our energy and return to the world refreshed. It is where we freely express who we are, where we transmit our values, and where we find comfort and solace. Our home is a temple where we meditate and practice presence as we cook, clean, play and work. Like the monastic in their monastery, we inhabit our temple with thoughtfulness and gratitude, attending to its maintenance with presence.

Listen to your home without judgment. What is it saying to you? Appreciate and use your home to create more joy in your life

WALKING WITH OUR FAMILIES

When I was a little girl my mother would wake up early in the morning to meditate and center herself while the family was still asleep. I'd snuggle down under the covers and listen to the quiet and calm. Pattering out to the kitchen when I heard her stir, I found a warm, centered mom and a home infused with the sweet invitation of incense. This was my first introduction to meditation. Although my mother's meditation scented our home, meditation wasn't something we did as a family. She never insisted that anyone in the family meditate. My father and older brother never did. When my younger brother and I became teenagers my mom offered to bring us places where meditation was taught. Fast forward years later and both my younger brother and I have become meditation teachers. Her example proved more powerful than she could have imagined.

Some people naturally share their spiritual practice with their families while others have a more private relationship with meditation. Sometimes one parent is not interested in meditating while the other treasures the practice. This has often been the case with the moms I've worked with over the years and was the case in my family. It's not necessary that our partner join us in practice. Giving the space for them to choose, or not choose, to meditate opens up the freedom for our loved ones to listen to their own inner wisdom. Just as we give ourselves the freedom to be who and where we are, we offer others the same freedom to be who and where they are. Each one of us sets foot on the path in our own way and in our own time.

It's natural to want to share something new and wonderful with others—especially family. But we need to be patient and trust that the right time and place will arrive, we just need to listen for it. Since meditation is an inner process it's not productive to proselytize or manipulate. It's easy to turn people off, and once that happens it's hard to reset to neutral and try again. Rather than telling people what we think is good for them, we can demonstrate the value of our practice through our actions and essence. Our family then comes to us when they are inspired to develop that same essence in their own lives. It becomes their idea to practice. They own it. In the meantime, the energy of our spiritual practice is having a powerful effect on our family even if they don't sit with us.

But if we choose to share meditation with our family there are some skillful ways to do this. Meditation is simple, and when put simply children can enjoy immediate benefits. I've seen children as young as four years old sit in meditation with Thich Nhat Hanh and walk mindfully with him through the forest. Offering a practice like meditation is a great gift to give a child, one that will serve them their entire lives. The introduction can be made fun by including books and games. One game my girls liked was putting glitter in a jar of water with a viscous liquid, like vegetable glycerin, shaking up the jar and inviting the child to sit very still and watch the glitter slowly settle to the bottom. That brings the child right into the present moment and gives them an immediate experience of calm.

Meditation engages the experiential side of spiritual practice while the wisdom side of practice can be engaged through stories. There are many wonderful wisdom stories from all around the world indigenous to various cultures. Reading to our children during quiet time infuses wisdom stories with a sense of well-being. The child's imagination develops while learning about different cultures, soaking up different perspectives and spiritual principles. A well told story makes us think *and* feel. It opens up a vast universe outside our little world. A story can enter deeply into our consciousness through the same door that music and poetry enter. Great teachers, like Jesus and the Buddha, taught spiritual principles through stories. Storytelling is a rich and delightful way to share our values with our family.

There are many ways to be a family and many ways to include family in our practice. The very best way is by becoming living examples. The most essential aspect of our family's spiritual education is our own full and sincere practice. Our family will notice and benefit from the calm we exude, whether or not they practice. They learn the value of meditation by noticing how it calms us, opens our heart, and enables us to listen with presence. Nothing is missed by those close to us, even when what they are absorbing goes unacknowledged. No need to seek confirmation of our effectiveness. The energy we create by our practice quietly and gently alters the entire ecosystem.

Being a woman and living the family life has been considered an impediment to awakening by many religious systems. But we need to remember that this verdict comes down from mostly celibate men who have not honed their practice in the fire of family life. When family life becomes our place of practice there is ample opportunity to develop selflessness as we care for others. Unconditional love arises as we give birth to a human so helpless they could not survive without our care, discipline arises from the need to feed others and see to their welfare day after day, regardless of how we feel. True, it is easy to stray into selfish attachment when we live the family life. But even monastic life has its challenges. Each path has its strengths and its pitfalls. The pitfalls can be approached as opportunities rather than impediments. Our challenge as practitioners on the family path is to develop focus and presence in the midst of constant activity, to not become tribal in our affections, to develop the capacity to love deeply and let go lightly and to continually broaden our perspective.

Allow your practice to be full and to infuse your family and home with its goodness. Open to ways to invite them in.

Standing

As we become more present during our sitting practice and in our daily life, a desire to support the awakening of the world naturally arises. The world needs the grounded sanity we are developing in our personal practice. Our awakenings help heal and move the larger community in a compassionate direction.

How do we stand up for our country, all living beings, and the planet while maintaining our spiritual practice? Like Martin Luther King Jr., Gandhi and others who have employed their spiritual practice to stand up for freedom, how do we stand our ground without becoming rigid, angry or hopeless?

I consider human rights work, or activism, to be a kind of spiritual practice. By defending those people who are persecuted for their race, religion, ethnicity, or ideology, you are actually contributing to guiding our human family to peace, justice, and dignity.

The 14th Dalai Lama

ACTIVELY PASSIVE

While standing in line at the post office it dawned on me that I might be stuck there for a long time. There were 10 people in front of me and only one postal employee. I wanted to leave, but the package had to be mailed. I saw three choices: I could leave and let the package arrive late, I could stay in line and be irritable, or I could stay in line and use the time to just be present. Planting my feet on the ground, I watched my mind resisting being where I was. It told me: *this is a waste of time, why is the woman talking so much to the postal employee? Why is the kid two people in front of me pulling out all the flyer envelopes and scattering them on the floor? Why, why, WHY?* I wasn't sure what was more boring and irritating— the circumstances or my mind. So I let my mind dump its contents out without commentary and continued to keep my two feet firmly planted on the ground. After a bit of time my mind exhausted itself and I was able to just stand. Everything became lighter and more spacious.

Although practicing presence while standing in line thankfully eases irritants, this is not the ultimate aim of standing meditation. The ultimate aim of standing meditation is to be fully present wherever we are. Resistance causes suffering—surrender is the antidote. The woman in front of the line coughs, the child runs up and down the aisles, the man behind me smells like onions. Nothing has changed in the outer circumstances. Meditation is not about creating our own private Eden in which everything is beautiful and fragrant. That is called spiritual bypassing—or using meditation to block out what we don't like—which is just another form of resistance. We may be able to cut off unpleasant sensations sometimes, but the unpleasant will eventually invade our perfect environment. When that happens, trying to block things out is apt to make us twice as irritable. Not only do unpleasant situations continue to arise, but now they threaten our well-earned calm!

Whether we're sitting, walking, standing, or lying down we have the opportunity to practice presence. All the lost moments- waiting in line moments, stuck in traffic moments, DMV moments, can be used as opportunities to practice everything we're learning about presence during our sitting meditation. We discover we can relax into just being where we are. Not only do we arrive at our destination in a better mood, we deepen our appreciation of life's fleeting opportunities. Stitch by stitch, we sew the moments of our life together with the thread of awareness.

Standing practice has a different texture than sitting practice. We don't usually stand in one place while at home or in private. Standing is usually a position taken in public. Standing practice also has a different texture than walking practice. Walking is active while standing is passive. The combination of both being in public and being passive makes standing a perfect place to explore the stance of an activist. When we stand with our two feet planted firmly on the ground, we are prepared to move, not rashly or impulsively, but with intention. We stand solidly in the present moment and are aware of our surroundings. We are poised to move, yet stationery and alert, like a cat watching a mouse from behind the sofa. This is how we practice standing meditation.

When you find yourself in line feel your feet on the ground

SHE WHO HEARS THE SOUNDS
OF THE WORLD

When Buddhism enters a new land it sheds aspects of its culturally derived language and social customs so that the core teachings are relatable to the people in the new culture. Traveling from India to China, monastic Buddhism met the more lay, family-oriented forms of Taoism and Confucianism. In that meeting the Indian male god of compassion, Avalokiteshvara, *the lord who looks down compassionately*, transformed into the female goddess Kuan Yin, *she who listens to the sounds of the world*. The image of a god who looks down compassionately became the less remote image of a goddess who is right here with us in the thick of life with all its messiness.

Another word for meditation, whether on or off the pillow, is *listening*. When we meditate we set aside judgment and listen to thoughts, feelings, sounds, and sensations without becoming attached to, or rejecting, what we are noticing. We become Kuan Yin hearing all the sounds of the world without picking and choosing. As we listen deeply to the sounds of the world during meditation, insights arise of their own accord. We don't think insights into existence, they are just a natural outcome of listening. These sounds have the power to change our perspective on life. Some of the sounds call us to action.

As meditation practice progresses there are a couple of insights reported by those who have taken a deep dive. One of these insights is awareness into, for lack of a better word—the inherent emptiness of all things. This idea of emptiness can be problematic for Westerners who liken emptiness to nihilism and detachment. But *this* emptiness is much more nuanced and vital. It is not a cold, dead emptiness but a vibrant, alive essence. It is the ground of life, the dark womb from where all things emerge. We imagine that we are solid and substantial but we are actually porous and in constant flux. This dissolution and reassembling of what appears to be solid has been confirmed by nuclear science. Emptiness is the space in which everything is dissolving and reassembling.

Although we may understand intellectually that all things are impermanent and inherently empty, applying this realization to our everyday life entails a profound shift in perspective. As we continue to embody our understanding of emptiness, bit by bit, imagined control is released and we relax into the way things are, more easily adjusting and even flowing with the constant flux of life. We start to live our lives with more freedom and less fear. Our actions in the world are just as important as when we believed things were substantial and we were in control, but we become less attached to results. Rather than leading to detachment from the cries of the world, insight into emptiness allows us to engage more deeply with the world since we have become more agile.

Our insight into emptiness is accompanied by the complementary insight into how all life is interconnected. This awareness of our interconnectedness is not unique to Buddhism. In Matthew 20:40 Jesus said, "inasmuch as ye have done it unto one of the least of these my brethren, ye have done it unto me. We are not at the top nor are we at the bottom of the heap. We all have our unique lives to live and unique contributions to offer. Insight into interconnectedness challenges the value of comparing our life to the life of others. This awareness naturally leads to confidence and to caring about the plight of others—humans, animals, plants and this beautiful planet we are fortunate to live on.

Activism is a natural outcome of awareness into emptiness and interconnectedness. The spiritual practitioner comes to activism through the compassion that organically arises out of these twin insights. As we progress on the path we realize that it is not enough to awaken by ourselves in the safety of our homes. We awaken in relation to the grasses, the snakes, the trees, the Koala bears and all other myriad forms of life. As they say in Bioneers, *it's all alive, it's all connected, it's all intelligent, it's all relatives.*

When I was a young student trying to decide which path to choose I asked my root teacher what she thought—should I marry and become a mother, dedicate my life to the practice and become a Buddhist nun, or pursue art as a life and career? She said, "If you were meant to be a nun there would be no question and what's one more painting in a museum?" She wasn't telling me that being a mother is more or less important than being an artist or nun, just that it's unwise to make life choices based on what will bring the greatest recognition. We humans crave permanence and recognition. The ego wants to feel special. We do not want to be just another grain of sand on the beach, just another mother washing dishes. When we evaluate ourselves as more or less important than others we remain a prisoner to our ego. We become more alienated and less able to hear the cries of a world.

Kuan Yin not only hears the sounds of the world, she engages with them. You can see this symbolized in statues of her as she holds a jar of healing water in one hand and a willow branch used to disperse the healing water in the other. Hers is an active form of love. In other statues, Kuan Yin has many hands, each one holding a different implement, providing her with an infinite variety of tools she can use to minister to those who are in pain. Different cries call for different forms of action. For some cries Kuan Yin writes, for some she offers medicine, for some she cooks, for some she sings, for some she applies bandages, for some she legislates. Kuan Yin is needed everywhere and in every field. Like a stone dropped into a stream our actions have a ripple effect. Even if we think our actions are futile, nothing is lost.

Before, during, and after acting, Kuan Yin listens. She listens to the birds in the fields, to the sirens on the street, to the children, the elders, the rich men and women, the poor men and women, the conservatives and the immigrants. Listening to the voices around us brings us into communion with our beautiful, complex, messy, interconnected world. While listening to the cries of those around us, arising compassion naturally leads to action. We are compelled to do our small part to mend the tear in the fabric of the world, healing both she who listens and that which is being heard.

Listen to your life without judgment

AN AUTHENTIC
LIFE OF JOYFUL SERVICE

When Zhao Zhou was asked, "What is meditation?", he answered, "It's not meditation." Well, then what is it? "It's alive! It's alive!"

We meditate in privacy and stillness then bring the practice into our everyday activities. As the practice develops it spirals out from our home coloring our actions in the wider world. Meditation's influence becomes larger than the calm and healing it thankfully brings. The practice connects us with the river running underneath our life. Once connected to the river of life the natural response is to want to nurture and preserve its waters.

The Zen word for someone who commits their life to service, putting aside their own complete enlightenment in order to bring all beings along with them, is bodhisattva. Put simply, a bodhisattva is someone who has dedicated themselves to supporting the awakening of others. This is the Zen orientation to selfless service. A bodhisattva is not out to convert anybody but to support the awakening of all beings regardless of their background or orientation. In the West we call those who act from a place of selflessness heroes or heroines. Bodhisattvas and heroes are both called into service by deep compassion emanating straight from their hearts.

We don't always recognize heroes and heroines because they come in all shapes and sizes. And they are not perfect people. Like the rest of us, heroes and heroines have their issues. What distinguishes them is their strong impulse to care for others and the courage and persistence they demonstrate in that active care. Although there are some heroes and heroines, such as Martin Luther King Junior or Ghandi, who give their life for the betterment of the whole, heroes and heroines are not always martyrs. Their service, though it may be challenging, can also lead to a deeply fulfilling life.

Many of us are called to serve selflessly in one way or another. When we get in touch with our unique talents and interests we discover the way Kuan Yin wants to work through us. We know her call by the sense that we are in the right place. When we follow our bliss, we are following the call of Kuan Yin. Whether we are called to make music, raise babies, crunch numbers, serve the homeless or anything else, what we do for the betterment of all is equally important. We are adding our unique and essential piece to the whole.

One of my personal favorite heroes is Fred Rogers, of *Mister Rogers Neighborhood*. Fred Rogers followed a calling to minister to children. He was a great listener and a great teacher of empathy and curiosity. A more unlikely, but equally as passionate, hero was Johnny Cash. Johnny Cash was called to minister to men in prison and bring the possibility of redemption and dignity into their lives. His approach of going into the prisons was both courageous and compassionate. Ruth Bader Ginsburg heard the call to uplift women in America, Mother Teresa ministered to the sick and dying all over the world, numerous people who risked their lives during the holocaust to shelter Jewish children, firefighters who run into burning buildings to save occupants—these are all selfless servants. An unlikely gathering!

Besides the famous heroes and heroines we know of, there are also many unsung ones. I have known nurse's aides who tenderly care for the elderly. These caregivers love the pace of the elders and the intimacy they enjoy with people who have lived a long life. They create the last taste of love for their patients. Most people will never know these caregiver's names but their simple lives are filled with richness and meaning and the work they do in the world is essential. Others find their calling in inventing technologies or programs that solve environmental problems, or sustainable farming, or reporting important information to the public. All activities are the work of selflessness when the impulse is to serve. A heroes' or heroine's hallmark is not so much what action they take as this impulse to service leading to actions that bypass thinking and emerge straight from the heart. Firemen don't think about whether or not it's a good idea to go into the building to save someone, they just follow their impulse and do it.

There's a special place in my heart for the selfless grandmothers, grandfathers, mothers and fathers who put off their own aims in order to work for the future success of their families, like Spike Lee's grandma who put away portions of her Social Security check each month to put him through college. They cook, they clean, they guide, and they work- sometimes 2 or 3 jobs, to provide the means necessary for their families to develop and eventually thrive. They move to far off lands where they don't speak the language so that their children may have a brighter future. They put aside their own dreams in order to nurture the dreams of the people they love. To say they have wasted their lives taking care of others dishonors the great service to humanity they selflessly offer.

Joseph Campbell coined the phrase- *follow your bliss*. Another way to say this is be your best self, live an authentic life. Sometimes it feels like we are choosing our calling and sometimes life pushes us into a calling we may not have imagined. However it shows up, we are each called to serve different populations in different ways at different times. If we listen closely to our life's circumstances we can discover our unique calling. The things that keep showing up and the things we are drawn to are good clues to our personal expression of joyful service. Our service may be local or it may be global. Size is of no consequence. The main thing is that we feel, in our bones, that we are living the life we are called to live and we are connected to, and uplifting, the whole in our own, unique way.

What brings you joy and enhances your community?

A LOTUS GROWS
OUT OF MUDDY WATER

Nancy was born out of wedlock to a teenage mother. On her first day of life, Nancy's mother left her at the doorstep of a church. She was soon adopted, but when she was eight years old her adoptive parents were killed in a car accident so she was moved to a foster home. It was there that the abuse began—sexual, physical and mental. Nancy endured the abuse for a number of years until it was discovered by a social worker and she was moved again, this time to a home with kind parents. I met Nancy when I was a foster mom. She had become a foster mom for numerous children, determined to give them what she had wanted so desperately when she was a young girl. Nancy was a great foster mother of many children. The experience of abuse gave her an ability to really understand what her foster children were feeling and needing in a way that I, who hadn't had that experience, could never offer them.

The lotus flower blooms out of muddy water. Without the mud the flower will not grow as full and fragrant. We are all born out of muddy water in this imperfect world where people we love die, where many are struggling to survive, some are struggling for meaning and many are desperately lonely. Even if we enjoyed a wonderful childhood, if we have an open heart it's hard to make sense of the pain we see and read about every day. This is the way it is—this is the atmosphere in which we are all awakening like lotus flowers out of our portion of pain included in the human experience.

Our parents are imperfect, our world is imperfect. Whatever our imperfect parents and imperfect world handed down to us is now our legacy—their work is over and ours has begun. The challenge set before us is to lift ourselves up out of any loneliness, fears, anger and addictions we are experiencing. When we cease blaming our parents or circumstances for these feelings, we can begin to rise up through the muddy water into the light. Our allotment of pain is not meaningless. It is the manure that nourishes the sweet bud of our flowering. Without pain how could we ever develop compassion?

Because we are embarrassed by our addictions, selfishness, anger, ignorance and greed it is tempting to try and hide these impulses, even from ourselves. But ignoring uncomfortable thoughts and feelings doesn't make them disappear. They grow in the darkness and seep out through the cracks. We're apt to project those rejected dark thoughts and feelings onto others— whether they are the people in our life or people from unknown cultures. Our world becomes a scary place when we project our negativity outwards. We see enemies everywhere because the real enemy remains hidden in the darkness, as close as our breath. Blaming others for our unhappiness is a large part of the world's dysfunctional history. This is the story of xenophobia, a story in which millions of innocents suffer everyday all over the world. If we are going to be peacemakers we first need to make peace with our own imperfect self.

Even wholesome activities, such as meditation and love for our family, can become toxic when they are tainted with a lack of self-awareness. Love for our family can turn into a tribal exclusion of others, meditation can turn into cold detachment or spiritual bypassing. I saw this in Burma where the generals who terrorize their people are often avid meditators and many have even been monks. Meditation alone does not make one a kind human being. A compassionate heart grows out of honesty about our very human anger, greed and ignorance. An essential aspect of awakening is born out of facing what we most want to run from. Not just once or twice but as a never ending inquiry. We expand our love and care further and further out to our community, our country, our planet and the universe. There is no escaping this and there is no shortcut. If we cease expanding and mistakenly believe we are fully awakened and beyond this at any point of the journey, our sense of identity is libel to harden and become toxic. This can happen to even the most advanced students and the finest spiritual teachers. Seeing the shadow in ourselves requires continual humility.

Awakening is a never-ending process, not a goal. Regardless of how long we've been on the path, we need to repeatedly take a courageous moral inventory of our strengths and weaknesses lest we delude ourselves into thinking we have arrived. By approaching awakening as a way of life, rather than something we have either attained or not attained, we can relax and enjoy the ride. At some point along the way, when we are living honestly and in the present, we see how everything we have been through, each painful trial and joyful windfall, adds up to our unique beauty and fragrance. We become grateful for the pain we've lived through. It is the dog barking at our heels, keeping us on the path.

Forgive yourself for perceived imperfections and blossom where you are

ANGER IN THE SERVICE
OF COMPASSION

Sitting by a cozy fire in the living room, reading a book and snuggling up on the couch wrapped in a blanket. The fire warms the autumn chill with tongues of dancing orange and yellow flames. Later that October evening, as the fire in the fireplace burnt down and I climbed into bed, something didn't seem right. The wind had a different feel. I lay sleepless, staring at the news on TV. The Sonoma firestorms were burning in neighborhoods to the north, east and south of my home. Fueled by unprecedented winds they quickly spread and raged out of control. When the smell of smoke started seeping into the house I knew it was time to throw some things in a bag and evacuate. Leaving my home, not knowing if I'd have a home to return to, driving through smoke and seeing the glowing red hills, I headed for the ocean.

Fire takes many forms. It has the power to warm and protect us and to cook our food. It also has the power to destroy our home and everything we've worked so hard to build. Like fire, anger also takes many forms. Anger can motivate us to speak up and set boundaries, impel us to protect ourselves and others. It can also fuel the destruction of our life and our relationships. Since we all experience our fair share of anger it behooves us to learn how to work with this vital force. Protectors of children, animals, and the vulnerable, need to become especially good stewards of anger. The fire of anger can become a valuable ally in the quest for fair and compassionate treatment of the Earth and all its life forms. But in order to harness this energy we first need to acknowledge, unconditionally and without shame, the anger we are feeling.

When I was in Burma with a group of meditators our host took us to a famous temple where pilgrims brought fruit, rice and other delectables to place at the feet of a large golden Buddha statue. Outside the gates of the temple sat dangerously thin women and children who were begging and selling trinkets. When I went to purchase a necklace from a mother and her young son my Burmese host slapped my hand away and told me not to encourage them. The anger I felt towards those who find it more spiritual to give food to an inert statue than to a living human being powers my work to this day. The anger is not at the Burmese people per se but at any system that encourages form over substance. This, and other inequalities towards women and children that I continually witness, is what made me become an activist and writer in support of women and children. If I did not acknowledge my anger, or if I wished it away, my life would have remained a self-centered life.

It's important to distinguish between rage, hatred, compassionate anger, and irritation. Rage is out of control and highly destructive like the wildfires that rampaged over the hills of Sonoma. Rage destroys everything in its path indiscriminately. Hatred is a long lasting seething that builds up energy over time like a snowball rolling down a mountain becoming ever larger and more powerful. Hatred feeds itself with each new perceived injustice. Out of rage and hatred vengeance is created. With vengeance we project our pain outwards and try to make others suffer as we are suffering. The Buddha likened this form of anger to picking up a hot coal and throwing it at the enemy. The coal may or may not hit the enemy but in the mean-time it is burning our own hand. Rage and hatred fester and can cause damage to our health and relationships. They are not extinguished by acting out. Only reflection and deep release can eventually calm the flames.

On the other hand, compassionate anger motivates us to act when presented with something that needs to change. Compassionate anger is what I felt when I saw the hungry mother and child begging for food while people were offering food to a statue. This sort of anger is like placing our hand on a hot stove. We feel the pain and quickly pull our hand away from the heat and out of harm's way. The pain isn't good or bad, it's just a signal that something needs to change. Compassionate anger is nature's way of telling us that something is amiss. It is our emotional immune system warning us of danger. This form of anger provides a flash of heat that encourages us to step into a situation we would otherwise avoid. It is the spark that starts the engine. Hopefully we step in wisely, but that we step in at all is thanks to compassionate anger.

The mildest form of anger is irritation. Irritation is anger looking for a place to happen. It's the feeling we experience when someone cuts us off in traffic or is late for a meeting or says something we don't like to hear. Irritation often has a physiological basis. When we don't get enough sleep, eat too much sugar or are physiologically imbalanced in one way or another we are more prone to irritation. These small embers can escalate if not tended. The embers of irritation burn themselves out during meditation and everyday mindfulness.

Blanket condemnation of an entirely natural feeling such as anger is unhealthy and counterproductive. Without anger we would most likely remain complacent in the face of cruelty, ignorance and greed. The powerful energy of anger is not only a call to action, like adrenaline it can provide fuel for the action required to set things right when they go off the rails.

Because of the power anger has to motivate us to affect a change, it can be threatening the status quo. Those who hold power may try to squelch or redirect our feelings of anger. These sorts of deflections have been used to control people throughout the world for ages. Men in power are socially permitted to express anger whereas when women express anger they are derided for being harsh and unfeminine and when unempowered minorities express anger they are called militant. Women and minorities who fight for equality are written off as angry, dangerous, and irrational in an attempt to shame them into being more docile. Focusing on the expression of anger as bad, rather than dealing with the source of the anger, is a clever deflection. It's helped keep women all over the world unempowered for centuries.

Although anger is great for calling us into action it is not always helpful once we've started acting. Unexamined anger can cloud our thinking and, rather than building bridges and helping to create more equitable systems, can become obsessive and self-perpetuating. When that happens, anger has outlived its usefulness and has devolved into a toxin. After receiving the message anger brings we need to let go of the emotional and physical charge left over from the burning. There is actually a physical component to that charge that needs to be released from the body. One way to release the physical component of anger is through vigorous physical activity. When I feel angry I become restless and agitated and find it difficult to sit in meditation. When this happens I switch to brisk walking meditation. Brisk walking is one way to safely release the physical charge left over from anger.

As our awakening unfolds we acknowledge and use the powerful force of anger wisely. If we try to deny anger, or shame ourselves for feeling angry, the emotion stagnates in dark pools within our psyche growing more and more dangerous to ourselves and others the longer it remains untended. Instead of either suppressing anger or mindlessly lashing out in rage we have the option to walk the middle path and use anger to affect a positive change. Anger can motivate us to get off our couches and move into the community in order to protect the vulnerable. Turning towards anger with unconditional attention we can hear what it is telling us then choose our actions wisely.

You are human, you experience anger. How do you deal with the anger you feel?

NOT KNOWING IS MOST INTIMATE

My friend Brittany met her husband at a bar. They had a fast, wild affair. A couple of months later she discovered she was pregnant so, still in the heat of infatuation, they married. Their marriage was a volatile one. Many nights I would wake up to a call from Brittany in tears asking me if she could spend the night, saying that her marriage was over. By the light of the next day they were back together. Thirty-five years later, their love is stronger than ever. Age has mellowed both of them. He adores her and she feels fortunate to be sharing her life with such a passionate, loving man. Brittany's relationship did not look like it would last. I gave it six months. Meeting at a bar, pregnant right away, both are alcoholics. Yet, although my husband and I were introduced by family, neither of us had substance abuse problems, we shared a common background, I practiced meditation, he made a great living as a professional psychologist, and we looked like a modern day Ken and Barbie, we only made it seven years while Brittany and her husband lasted a lifetime. This was an important and humbling lesson for me, one that I draw from whenever I think I know what is best. I'm no longer so sure of what I think I know.

There is a Zen koan that goes:

Not knowing is most intimate.

Our practice begins with not knowing. We sit in meditation, wash the dishes and make the bed without preconceived ideas about the moment. The moment unfolds and we unfold with it. We listen, we watch. As we listen and watch we become closer, more intimate, with our surroundings. In Zen another word for awakening is intimacy. While awakening we are becoming intimate with whatever the present moment holds. The contrived identity we use to distance ourselves from the unpredictable nature of life slowly dissolves. We enjoy a freshness of direct communion with our surroundings.

As children we are taught to learn the *right* answer. When we don't know the *right* answer we feel ashamed. We are taught that our religion, our philosophy and our politics are right and if someone doesn't agree with us they are wrong or misguided. Admitting to not knowing goes against the grain of everything we have been taught since childhood, threatening our hard-wired self-concept. It takes courage to question what we think we know- but the rewards are great. When we return to not knowing we return to our original child's mind, a mind full of wonder, curiosity, and aliveness where anything is possible. Once we get over the hump of feeling shame for not knowing and move into the openness and freedom that comes with meeting each moment fresh, the world opens up unlimited delights and possibilities.

When preparing to move into action in the world we feel like we know what is right and that we are going to move the situation in the right direction. We think we know the best way to parent, the best way to keep a house, to vote, to choose a mate or—we may think other people know what's right and we're clueless. As our practice develops over time, although we are still firm in our commitment to choose compassion over fear, we're not always so sure that our way is the only way.

When someone approaches us believing that they know what is right and that they are going to convince us to see things their way, we are liable to be resistant. But if someone approaches us with openness to our perspective, shows us respect, and is genuinely interested in us, we are more likely to be open to them. By loosening our white-knuckle grip on what we believe to be true we open up space for others to have their perspectives. Then we can really meet them where they are and intimacy is possible.

Not knowing is a wonderfully useful practice as we move into activism. As activists we are in the business of healing divides. Healing divides requires a sincere openness to all points of view. We want to understand what shapes another person's beliefs, what their concerns are. We want to listen carefully and learn about their hopes and fears. It is from a base of not knowing that we can begin to build bridges with others and experience fruitful connections. Then real change can happen, one person at a time.

Open yourself up to someone who believes differently than you

TO SHE WHO MUCH IS GIVEN

If you are reading this it is likely that you have a place to sleep tonight, food to eat, and some degree of safety. It is also likely that you live in a country that allows women to go to school, read, write, express their viewpoints and exercise the power to vote. We are most fortunate. There are many who have none of these things, who have been forced to leave their countries due to war or lack of opportunity and are seen as pariahs in strange lands. Within our borders are families living paycheck to paycheck just trying to survive, children and parents unable to afford a home to live in, teenagers incarcerated for lack of bail money. These struggling families are our families. As our practice develops, the division between "them" and "us" narrows and *their* happiness becomes our happiness, *their* pain becomes our pain. A deep yearning for all others to be free and awakening does not need to be mandated. Compassion naturally arises in an awakening mind.

People sometimes have a romantic view of spiritual practice that involves sitting in a quiet peaceful setting with incense burning while responding to all situations with equanimity. This is partially true— we do develop more calm, and there are times of great peace. But if this internal respite is not followed by bringing the calm we develop in our meditation into the world to help ease the suffering of others then our practice is nice—but just nice. It doesn't go much further than that. An unchallenged, untested calm is a shallow calm. The practice of awakening continues on as we move into the fray.

As our heart opens ever wider and we feel called to do something about what we see, we need to remain aware of our limitations and unique talents. We may feel helpless or even guilty for our good fortune. But feeling guilt or shame is not helpful to anyone. Instead, we can calibrate our activities so that we take care of ourselves, our families, our communities, and beyond without burning out. Meditation practice, as we move out into the world, can help us find balance in our giving. During meditation practice we become more aware of our body and mind. Listening to our body and mind with unconditional attention we notice when we are tired, when we are energized, when we need to back off from giving, and when we need to lean in. With awareness we can determine if a task is more than we can handle at the time and let go of guilt if it is not ours to do.

In this media-connected world, awakening to the pain of others can feel overwhelming. It's painful to sit idly by when others are suffering. On my desk are letters soliciting donations from global projects, local food and housing non-profits, political campaigns, and other worthy causes. All of them are important, but I can't possibly give money to every cause each time they solicit. In order to not become overwhelmed I pick one cause and write them a check when I sit down to pay my bills. When my coffers are full I give more and when there is less I give less—but I always give something. This old school system has worked for me for decades.

There is no end in sight to human suffering. There is no political system, no economic system, no religious system that will eliminate all greed and fear from the human psyche. We need to settle in for a lifetime of caring, a lifetime of voting, and a lifetime of giving what we can for the well-being of the planet and its inhabitants. At times we will feel like we are getting nowhere. We just keep putting one foot in front of the other. Caring for the world is a marathon, not a sprint.

In order to live a sustainable life of service it's useful to feel engaged by using our unique talents, to find ways to express ourselves, and remember to enjoy the process while staying attuned to our ever-shifting energy levels. It is essential to keep up our strength, to take good care of our body and personal lives in order to give wisely with an open heart. As people who feel the interconnectedness of life we learn how to live with a broken heart, it's just part of being human.

But we're of no use to others if our backs are broken. We are part of an ever-growing team of amazing people who are aware and living from a place of interconnection. Find your team and go for it!

Rest, recharge, and get back in there

Lying Down

We ground our lives through our private meditation practice, walk that awareness into our daily lives, and develop our practice while standing for those who need our support. All this is done with a warm heart, with the wish to create more kindness and sanity in our lives and the lives of others.

Yet, there are important aspects of life which we don't create, which we are not fully in control of. Aging, illness, and dying all challenge us to surrender control. How do we make peace with the ephemeral nature of life? How do we let go of our need to be in control and allow ourselves to flow with the tides? This section is about practicing in the midst of that which we cannot control.

We do not have to wait for the painful death of someone close to us or the shock of terminal illness to force us into looking at our lives. Nor are we condemned to go out empty-handed at death to meet the unknown. We can begin, here and now, to find meaning in our lives. We can make of every moment an opportunity to change and to prepare—wholeheartedly, precisely, and with peace of mind—for death and eternity.

Sogyal Rinpoche

WHEN WE HAVE NOTHING
LEFT TO GIVE

There are times in our lives when sitting, walking, or standing aren't options. Sometimes we are just too sick, sometimes our heart is too heavy, our mind is too stressed or too jumbled, and we can't bring ourselves into the present moment on our own steam. Often, when we need meditation the most, when we are looking down a dark tunnel—alone, struggling to just hang on—help feels unreachable. When we feel hopeless or exhausted we need different resources than the resources we use when we're up on our feet. This is when an imaginative practice can be a lifesaver. Imagination has the ability to reach into the mystery and throw us a lifeline we can hang on to till we're back up on our feet again.

Everybody goes through hard times, it's part of the human experience and nothing to be ashamed of. I have experienced many dark days and nights when my heart was broken and I couldn't see my way out of a painful present. During these times I've learned to use special techniques to help focus my awareness. I am forever grateful for practices that have allowed me to walk through my personal hells with curiosity. During one such difficult time I was studying with a Theravadin monk from Sri Lanka whose name was Bhante Punnaji. Before becoming a monk, Bhante Punnaji was a physician, well known for his healing abilities. Bhante taught me a body sweeping meditation that helped facilitate greater ease in my body when I was feeling tight and stressed. Here is the body sweeping meditation Bhante Punnaji shared:

Lie down in a comfortable position. Starting at the feet, focus on any sensations in the feet without judgment, accepting whatever is found there. Rather than trying to avoid or contract around the sensations, repeat, "My feet are strong and healthy".

Here's where the imagination comes in:

Picture your feet as strong, and healthy while focusing gently on any sensation in the area. Stay in that area as long as you like repeating this until you sense a glimmer of ease in your feet. Then move up to the shin/calf area and bring that same affirmation and awareness there. Keep going up the body ending at the head. You can take as much, or as little, time as you like. Once the whole body has been mentally swept, go back to the feet and start again, or begin a general body awareness meditation, or move back into your day.

When I was pregnant I discovered a key to this body sweep meditation in a book called *Spiritual Midwifery*. In this book Ina May Gaskin recommends thinking of birthing sensations as "strong" rather than painful. The thought of pain creates fear in the mind whereas the thought of a strong sensation is easier to approach with curiosity. It's natural to contract around pain. Reframing the sensation as strong, rather than painful, creates some space around the experience, space in which the sensation can be explored without pulling away or tightening up. This has been a valuable bit of information for my practice.

Another useful imaginative practice is guided meditation. Sometimes, when practicing on our own is too difficult, we need to rely on others to meditate for us. During these times, guided meditation can be a friend, taking us on a journey and inviting us to look at life with fresh eyes. When I was sick for a long stretch of time there were days I didn't have the capacity to focus enough to read or watch TV let alone to meditate. But I was able to listen to meditation tapes. Each day, often a number of times a day, I would lie down, wrap myself in a blanket, and let a guided meditation wash over me. I'd sink into the clarity of the speaker's voice and let it carry me to a brighter world. These guided meditations were lifesavers when I had difficulty concentrating. They opened me up to a more expansive world than the one I was experiencing. A guided meditation can speak our meditation for us.

We are attempting to create a through-line of meditation in our lives. Through clear, joyful times, through dark confused times, through neutral times, we keep walking. Sometimes it's difficult, sometimes it's ecstatic, and sometimes we're just walking. I don't know where I'd be now without the lifelines that were thrown out to me when I was unable to carry my own weight. At the very least, my life would be shallower and I would be a more fearful person. I have learned that, regardless of what situations or states of mind a person is in, they can become lighter, see further, and relax more deeply into the moment thanks to the practice.

Find a teacher you trust and allow yourself to sink into their guided meditation

CONSCIOUS AGING

As challenging as the early years of parenting may be, many parents will remind a young mother or father to savor the early years with their children because the time goes by so quickly. Before you know it the baby is walking across the living room floor, then saying no, then going to school, then caring more about their friends than their embarrassing family, then moving out to start their young adult life. Just when you figure out one stage they're onto the next. This advice—to savor each stage—is useful regardless of what stage of life we're in. Life goes by quickly for all of us, from the first tooth to the first car, to the first kiss, to the first job, to the first child, to the first gray hair. When we live each stage with presence, the gnarly sleepless nights become just part of the adventure.

Each leg of our journey has its delights and its challenges. When we are children, we enjoy less responsibility but also have less power. Life is happening to us. As we blossom into our teen years everything seems possible, we see through hypocrisy and may even feel invincible, but we often lack the power and experience to wisely guide our ship. In early adulthood we are at our physical peak. We are finally in charge of our lives! We have power, but it comes with lots of responsibilities. As we age we watch our body slowing down, our skin becoming thinner, our hair whiter. We feel more aches and pains as we say farewell to our youth. There's no way around it—life is bittersweet. But the substantial wisdom we've gained by living our life with presence enables us to guide others and support the generations coming up behind us. We can look over our life's landscape and see wide and far. If we've been aware and letting go along the way there is a delightful simplicity available to us. We need less than we thought we needed.

Conscious aging is worlds apart from unconscious aging. If we live our life without awareness, undigested bits of experience accumulate leaving more and more toxic residue throughout our psyche. The older we get the greater the accumulation of toxins. Siddhartha, later to become a Buddha, discovered an antidote to accumulating toxins. After seeing an old man, a sick man and a dead body he was shocked into the awareness that these three fates were part and parcel of every human life. He vowed right then and there to find a way out of this painful situation. He then saw a homeless monk and left his father's palace. Relinquishing a life of luxury, he set off to search for a cure to human suffering. Walking out past the palace gates, young Siddhartha entered the homeless life.

What Siddhartha discovered as a homeless seeker, after much trial and error, was not a path leading to the end of pain, but a path leading to the end of suffering. Pain is an intrinsic part of being human, but suffering is more pliable. Realizing how attachment creates suffering, the Buddha taught the power of non-attachment. This does not mean we do not have preferences or that we do not love deeply. It means we develop the capacity to let go, even when it is challenging to do so. It's easy to become attached to pieces of our life along the way, especially to our youth, our strengths, and the people we love. We even become attached to our pain, believing that the pain we've experienced is essential to who we are. We crave permanency in a world that is governed by the natural law of impermanence. The tighter we cling, the greater our suffering.

During meditation we witness impermanence up close and personal. Each moment brings a host of emerging and dissolving thoughts, feelings, and sensations. We watch as each thought, feeling, and sensation comes into view then fades into the nothingness from which it arose. No matter how beautiful or ugly, good or evil, a thought or sensation may seem, it is impermanent. That's great news when it comes to the painful, uncomfortable thoughts and sensations we dislike, but not such good news when it comes to the warm, delightful sensations we cling to.

During meditation we create a safe space where we can relax into letting go of both uncomfortable *and* comfortable sensations. We watch everything changing before our mind's eye. Impermanence transforms from an interesting concept into something we actually experience. Slowly, bit by bit, we develop a comfort and facility with constant change by watching the coming and going of each breath, each thought, and each feeling. Our suffering diminishes as we loosen our white-knuckle grip of attachment and let go of our fear of change. Then, we may feel sad when our child grows up and leaves the nest, but notice that the change affords us more time to explore passions we have put aside. We may lose our youthful bodies, but we've gained a wisdom and comfort with the body we have lived in all these years. People we love die and new people and communities rise up to support us. Our face becomes the face we've created through years of smiling, tears, and laughter. We enjoy well-earned wisdom and deep connections with others. We come to appreciate the small things.

We are apt to become bitter and dry as we age if we don't process our portion of the pain life doles out. The antidote is meeting both the pain and the joy with honest, authentic awareness. Our mind remains fresh when we live in the present moment. We become less concerned with what other people think of us, less bitter about those who wronged us, less regretful over lost opportunities. Former hurdles we've conquered morph into nuggets of wisdom that we can share with others. The more challenges we've faced and lived through with awareness, the deeper our wisdom and the more we have to share.

Conscious aging burns off the small stuff revealing a deeper life purpose. In place of youthful ambition we are left with delight in a crisp apple, a good night's sleep, a maple tree changing colors with the seasons, the warmth of a child curled up on our lap, and the joy of giving back. We have more to offer future generations and the planet. All the stages we've moved through become available to us. We are fresh and creative like a child, experimental and honest like a teenager, productive and in charge like an adult, and wise like an elder.

Embrace your current stage and enjoy each change as it comes

STILLNESS AND ILLNESS

When I was struck down with a strange debilitating illness in my thirties the diagnosis of Chronic Fatigue Syndrome (CFS) did not exist. The temporary name for the illness that was consuming my energy was the "yuppie flu". The doctor told me that what I needed to do was join *Parents without Partners*. I spent most of my thirties, and much of my forties, trying to figure out what was wrong with my body and mind while raising my daughter as best I could as a single mother with very little family or community support. It came to the point where all I could do was drag myself out of bed, get my daughter to school, drive home, get back into bed, doze and look out the window until it was time to pick her up. I had to drop out of graduate school and leave a job I loved requiring us to tighten the belt once again.. Dating? I don't think so.

I could no longer live my life how I wanted to live it-advancing in my work and education, enjoying leisure time in the garden or my art studio, sitting down with Nicole as she practiced piano, driving her to extracurricular activities, developing a career, hanging out with friends, and starting a new family. I had held tight to the vision of being a fully engaged mother and, although this is a wholesome goal, and heaven knows I tried my best to implement it, life had other plans. I became exhausted fighting with life over my unrealized plans. There was nowhere to turn, no way out. Lying in bed, I surrendered and let whatever it was take me wherever it wanted to take me.

Most of us have a picture in our mind of how we want our life to unfold. That's natural. Plans and dreams can propel us forward. But when do dreams and drive turn into willfulness? How do we know when to keep pushing and when to let go? When we fight what we can't control we just create more pain and suffering for our family and ourselves. I was fortunate to be engaged in a practice that guided me—in a practical and deep way—towards letting go of willfulness.

In her charming book, *The Sound of a Wild Snail Eating,* Elizabeth Tova Bailey writes about her plunge into the depths of debilitation. During the worst of it she was forced to leave her forest home and move into a small apartment near the hospital. A friend had picked up a snail from Elizabeth's beloved forest and placed it in an aquarium for her. At first this seemed odd to Elizabeth but as time went on she became fascinated, even in love, with this snail. He (she? it?) became the center of her world. Elizabeth was unable to move from her bed, even to get a drink of water, but she could still have companionship and witness an entire world as it unfolded, all thanks to the little snail.

When CFS was at its worst, I lay in bed for hours looking out at the weeds and mountains and sky through my bedroom window. There I discovered a magical parallel world I had been too busy to notice before. It was full of mockingbirds, and green grasses swaying in the wind, spindly legged spiders, drifting clouds that were sometimes angry and sometimes playful, and a carpet of tiny blue flowers underneath the almond tree. It was beautiful beyond description. This little window world was precious to me and I felt a profound sense of gratitude for it.

Bit by bit I reentered the conventional world. As I returned I became curious about this life-transforming syndrome and interviewed others who had also pulled themselves out of a downward spiral. What they had to say was interesting. All of them reported that CFS had rendered their will impotent. They felt like they no longer had control of their life and most of them raged against this turn of events. They only began to recover after they finally surrendered to the limitations they were experiencing. What was unexpected was their gratitude for this illness that brought them closer to their lives, more appreciative of the small moments. They expressed a tremendous joy in the freedom that followed their surrender. Their experience was very much like mine. Life had taken the reins out of my hands and I encountered a bigger, more interesting reality. I reentered the busy world fundamentally changed. Suleika Jaquad, who has been in and out of Cancer treatment since her early 20's writes, "I've been thinking recently that the people I admire most are not those who bend reality to their will, but who accept it and find creative ways to engage with it. I think that's my definition of resilience: to accept what's happening moment to moment, and to allow for necessary adjustments, to pivot, to find relief, to cultivate small joys."

One of the many gifts CFS, in combination with spiritual practice, granted me was the gift of learning to trust the unfoldment of life, regardless of appearance. I began to watch, listen, and follow the trajectory of my life and became less attached to how I thought things should be. I still made plans but was more flexible when circumstances called for something different. What a relief to understand, deep in my bones, that I am not responsible for controlling the Universe, not even my small corner of the Universe. I am only responsible for what is in front of me right now—pay the bills, make dinner, love, paint, vote, go to the market, do what I can to help others, and feel what I feel.

I am once again pruning my rose bushes and planting tomatoes. My second family turned out to be my granddaughter who I am enjoying fully. I sit down each evening with Nai'a as she practices piano. I have what I visioned decades ago, although it is not how and when I thought it would show up. Each world has its magic and beauty, the world of the gardener who smells the earth as she works the soil, the world of a sightless person who is so sensitive to sound she can hear the beginning, middle, and end of a cat's footsteps, the world of the easy limbed walker trekking over mountains with a pack on her back, and the world of the person unable to walk who wonders at the spider as it spins its web.

Each world is precious; each world has different challenges and rewards. When I was forced to release my will about how I thought my life should go I came to appreciate a larger, more radiant life, a life that doesn't depend on circumstances for a sense of well-being and happiness. It, instead, offers worlds within worlds within worlds, each glowing, each wondrous. When one world dissolves another world appears.

When you feel sick, surrender and open to your life as it is right now

DEATHING

My dear friend lost her daughter to cancer this week. I sat with both of them throughout the transition, watching as they clung to survival and as death tore any hope of survival from their grasp. Two young children and a bereft husband were left behind. Now I sit with my friend as she grieves the loss of her daughter and takes over the job of being a mother figure to her two grieving grandchildren.

While grieving the death of his child the Zen master Kobayashi Issa was asked why, with all his depth of wisdom about the arising and passing of all things, did he still grieve. His response was:

It's a dew drop world, and yet…

Although we all know, on some level, that everything is impermanent, no matter how deep our practice may be, we still grieve at the loss of a loved one.

Daily survival was more grueling for our ancestors who faced death daily as they struggled to eat and not be eaten. We think we have conquered that struggle and forget that we too are tied up in daily survival. Accidents, illness, aging, a child killed in war, abandonment, sudden changes in our economic situations—we think of these as exceptional experiences that invade our otherwise fluid lives, but vulnerability is woven into the fabric of the human condition in these fragile human bodies we inhabit.

It's understandable to be in denial about the inevitability of death and somehow, magically, think it won't happen to us. As the founder of *Attitudinal Healing*, Dr. Gerald Jampolsky said "Almost everyone dies." In our death-phobic culture we are compelled to deny death's existence. When we do think about death we see it as tragic rather than as a natural part of every life. This makes us ill prepared for death when it inevitably comes knocking on our door. We wake up, tumble out of bed, open the shutters, feed the cat, make everyone breakfast, go to work. The day goes on like this, with one responsibility after another. The next morning we wake up and do a variation of the same thing all over again never thinking this could be our last day on Earth. It's easy to feel as if this routine will go on forever. But impermanence is a natural part of life. Before our life is turned upside down by change, we can put ourselves at an advantage by courageously facing our feelings about death. Our awareness becomes a super power when death arrives, making our ability to adjust to death more relaxed.

When I was a little girl I woke up in fear one evening. Leaving my warm bed, I climbed on to my father's lap and told him I was feeling scared. He asked what I was afraid of? My father, being a lawyer, brought me through a process of questions that narrowed the fear down to its essential elements. What we discovered at the core of my fear was the ultimate loss of control—death. While holding me safely in his arms, my father said, "Death is either a great adventure or the end of everything. Either way, it's not something to fear." These words have stayed with me and soothed me through many trials. They soothe me still.

There are numerous theories about what happens after we die—heaven and hell, reincarnation, complete extinction. What do you believe happens after death? Is it even important to know? We tend to believe what the people we trust tell us, but most of us don't really know, in our bones, what happens after we die. Different religions espouse different perspectives but few of us are certain that what we've learned from our native religion is really true. Some people turn to science for answers, but science doesn't have a lot to say about what happens after visible, quantifiable, signs of life cease. Some believe that when visible signs of life are no longer present nothing is left. Although this view masquerades as scientistic, it is a rather narrow and materialistic point of view about the end of life. It assumes that if we can't see it, it doesn't exist.. This is not good science. There are many cases of people having past life recall which have been verified by knowledge of things and places not encountered in this life. Even with this evidence, some still do not keep the exploration of the possibility of life after death open. Exploring the question of what happens after death is a personal journey, one each of us must walk for ourselves. Even though we may not come to any conclusion as to what happens after death, our exploration can help us face death and relax into the mystery.

There is a story about the Buddha being approached by a grieving mother. The mother carried her dead child around town desperately looking for a reprieve from her misery. She came to the Buddha, pleading with him to revive the limp baby in her arms. "Bring me a mustard seed from a home that has never known grief and I will revive your child," was the task the Buddha set before the grieving mother. The woman went from home to home asking for a mustard seed and in each home she heard stories of loss and grief. She returned to the Buddha saying "There is no one in this village who has been spared grief." While sharing in the pain of others, the grieving mother realized that she was not alone, that death comes to everyone. She went on to bury her child and follow the Buddha into the deathless realm.

It was a blessing to be able to support both my parents as they died in my home. I credit the time I spent thinking about death with giving me the ability to provide comfort for them as they were dying. Being there as someone is dying has some of the same magic as being there when someone is being born. The insignificant melts away and you meet life in its purest form. It is hard work but with the help of hospice it can be a deep, rich experience. Right after my father took his last breath he was glowing. This hard-nosed lawyer became pure love. I would not have seen this if I was pushing death away.

When we are faced with our mortality our life and practice gain urgency. What do we want to do with this short precious time we've been allotted? Spending time on petty disputes and concerns becomes less important. There is more richness in using our time to deepen our love and awareness and leaving something beautiful behind us when we go. The twin gifts that come with facing death—the release of fear and the added urgency to practice while we still can—help us relax into that which we cannot control and add fuel to our awakening process. Each moment, each life, is known to be precious.

When the Buddha lay dying in a forest grove in Kushinagar, surrounded by 500 disciples, his last words to them were,

It is in the nature of all things that take form to dissolve. Strive with your whole being to awaken.

Explore your feelings about death

GRADUAL AWAKENING

After about 15 years on the path as a dedicated practitioner I thought my life would fall into place. It was discouraging to see myself act out the same old patterns, the same old addictive behaviors, after working so diligently for so long. I questioned why I spent so much time and energy on meditation, reading spiritual literature, practicing generosity and gratitude, and all the other practices I so avidly pursued. If they didn't produce results, why was I bothering?

Forty plus years later I see that all the work I've been doing has slowly, wave by wave, eroded the cliffs of my patterns, negativities, and addictions. The patterns are still there but they no longer run my life. What I couldn't see 15, 20, or 30 years into the process was that this is a gradual path—that it takes patience and persistence.

What I wished someone had shared with me, what I want to share with you, is the value of accepting the many imperfections and bumps along the way. Life knocks us down, we take a deep breath, regroup, dust ourselves off, and recommit to our life and our practice once again. It's most helpful to see this work as a process rather than a goal and find ways to buckle up and enjoy the ride—because it sometimes feels like a long one. There is progress, although at times the progress isn't apparent. It's much more enjoyable if we commit to being in it for the long haul and release attachment to seeing immediate results. And there are many, many gifts along the way.

The heroine's journey is riddled with challenges. There are dead end roads, crevasses, and numerous temptations. It takes grit to walk this path, a path that runs contrary to the materialistic life laid out by society. There are many times when we have to choose one or the other, and it is not always an easy choice. It is each of these challenges, each of these choices that make our journey a heroine's journey.

So I wish you courage and persistence on your unique path. Find the rare and wonderful people who can support you, cherish these friendships. Keep yourself inspired by the words of the many heroines and heroes who have walked the path before you and left traces like breadcrumbs for you to follow. Make the path your own and share it with others.

May you enjoy many blessings along the way

www.ingramcontent.com/pod-product-compliance
Lightning Source LLC
Chambersburg PA
CBHW051540120626
46551CB00013B/1315